GAME BIRDS & GUN DOGS

by

Vin T. Sparano
Editor-in-Chief
Outdoor Life

Book 2 in the Outdoor Adventure Library
by Larsen's Outdoor Publishing

Copyright (c) 1992 by Vin T. Sparano

ISBN 0-936513-31-4

Library of Congress 92-74328

Published by:

LARSEN'S OUTDOOR PUBLISHING
2640 Elizabeth Place
Lakeland, FL 33813

PRINTED IN THE UNITED STATES OF AMERICA

1 2 3 4 5 6 7 8 9 10

DEDICATION

To my grandaughter "Gina Girl". I promise to show her all that I cherish in the outdoors and I know she will love these gifts as much as I.

ABOUT THE AUTHOR

Vin T. Sparano, Editor-In-Chief of Outdoor Life magazine, has hunted throughout the world. A lifelong devotee and collector of classic outdoor literature, his interests have blended ideally with his career at Outdoor Life, beginning in 1960. In addition to his magazine work, Sparano has written numerous books, columns and features for many national publications, including a weekly nationally syndicated outdoor column for Gannett News Service.

Sparano is also the editor of Hunting Dangerous Game, The Greatest Hunting Stories Ever Told, Classic Hunting Tales and Tales Of Woods And Waters.

CONTENTS

INTRODUCTION

I like bird hunting...but I love bird hunting with a dog. I often wonder what it would be like to hunt over a true field champion, a dog that performs flawlessly...a dog that locks on point when there is really a bird there...a dog that's steady to wing and shot...a dog that will drop the bird gently in your hand and not 10 yards away, where he may well gulp your quail down in one swallow.

If you have hunted over such a dog, you are lucky. I have not been so lucky. My dogs have bumped birds, run off to hunt on their own, refused to retrieve, and have otherwise frustrated and embarrassed me in the field. I suspect most hunters have been just as unlucky as I, but they just won't admit it. You can talk about a man's mother, wife and children, but don't dare imply that his dog is uncontrollable. You may never be invited to hunt birds with him again.

My first bird dog was Patch, a German Shorthair. Patch turned out to be a super bird dog, but I was too dumb to recognize it. I simply expected too much from Patch. I can recall one hunt when Patch pointed a pheasant across a 10-yard wide frozen drainage ditch. I couldn't see the bird in the snow across the ditch, so I started throwing snowballs. Eventually, the pheasant flushed and I dropped it across the ditch. By this time, several gun club members had stopped to watch. If Patch embarrasses me one more time, I thought to myself, I would take an oath not to feed him for six months.

I did not have to worry. Patch took a flying dive onto the ice, crashed through it, and proceeded to swim to the other side, breaking the ice with his paws all the way. When he got to the

9

opposite bank, he picked up the pheasant, jumped again into the icy water and swam back to me. Patch put the bird in my hand and in front of my hunting buddies, who are usually unmerciful in times of crisis. I will never forget that day, when my dog made me so very proud.

Did Patch turn out to be a champion? Not a chance! Two weekends after that flawless ice exhibition, Patch ran off our club land and onto a crowded trap field where a registered tournament was in progress. The event was stopped while I tried to coax Patch off the field in front of a crowd of spectators. My wife knew something was wrong when I returned home and nearly crushed a coffee mug in my hand.

Patch was good, and I shot hundreds of birds over him, but there were also times when he nearly drove me to drink. My problem was that I was comparing Patch to some field trial champions. I was impressed with the soldier-like performance of these dogs and I expected the same from Patch. But I never got it because Patch was a gun dog. He found birds for me. He broke point because the birds were running. He wasn't steady to wing and shot because he wanted to be under that bird when it came down. Cripples did not get away. Patch was a determined gun dog that lacked style in the field...but we always brought home pheasant dinners. I had hunted with a champion...I just didn't know it at the time.

Sandy, a little Brittany Spaniel, was the next gun dog to come into my life. Realizing that I may have been responsible for Patch's shortcomings, I sent Sandy to a trainer. About a week after I dropped her off, I got a call from the trainer. Sandy had flunked out! Her report card said "too immature." I decided to train her myself, thinking I had made all my mistakes with Patch. Naturally, I was wrong.

I can recall one session in the field when I decided to find out what my loyal gun dog would do if I suddenly suffered a heart attack. When Sandy wasn't looking, I fell to the ground and faked a coronary. I had visions of Sandy running 20 miles to summon help for her fallen master. She would tirelessly lead rescuers back to my fallen body, and I would be saved. Sandy would be famous and get huge cash prizes from dog food companies. But this never happened. When Sandy saw me, she lay down and went to sleep at my side.

Did Sandy turn out to be a good bird dog? I wouldn't want her to know that I told you this, but she's only fair to middlin'. But Sandy is something else. She is one of my best friends and follows me wherever I go. When I leave the house, Sandy watches from the window as I drive off. In fact, Sandy is curled up at my feet as I write this. Sandy will never be a champion, but she's my dog, so don't say anything bad about her.

Patch and Sandy are two very important reasons I compiled this collection of bird hunting and gun dog stories. There are few hunting experiences that match a day in the field with our dogs. At high noon, you will share your lunch with your dog and wonder what you will do after he's gone. Will your next dog be as good...or better? If you're a bird-dog man, you know these thoughts are inevitable and weigh heavily on your heart.

The stories here are about hunters, their dogs, and the upland game and waterfowl they hunt. These tales are about those remarkable shots...and unexplainable misses.

You will read about good gun dogs and heartbreaking dogs, but never about bad dogs...because there ain't no such animal. Read them all, then take your dog hunting. Share your peanut butter sandwich with him, and love him...even if he does run off and get lost.

Vin T. Sparano
Editor-in-Chief
Outdoor Life

1

THE COHUTTA GOBBLER

By Charles Elliott

Nearly all turkey hunters, without exception, are nuts. They have embraced this comparatively new game bird and made it a major influence in their lives. How many other hunters have you heard practice their game calls in offices, bars, parties, or wherever they may gather? Not many, I bet. These turkey hunters also attribute great feats of intelligence to the turkey, which may or may not be justified. And when a turkey gets away from them, it becomes a very special turkey and one that must be challenged. It even gets a name: Ghost Gobbler of Oak Ridge, or something like that. These hunters now become slightly irrational (or nuts) as they take up this special challenge. And my old friend Charlie Elliott, one of the finest turkey hunters in America, is no different from the rest of us. He regularly goes ape over a gobbler. Here's his tale of "The Cohutta Gobbler," a bird that gave him his greatest turkey hunt.

From the time of man's creation until he steps beyond the shadows, his life is not so much a matter of years, or seasons, or days as it is of moments. A vast majority of these are so vapid and humdrum that the mind makes no attempt to file them away in its incredible storehouse. Many others remain as memories or facts available to our mental computers. A few of the latter stand out bright and vivid and, in spite of the years, never lose one sparkle of their original brilliance or beauty.

One of those highlights in my life had to do with a wild turkey-gobbler. I have avoided saying "the" highlight for fear of domestic or other repercussions, but my moment of grandeur with that magnificent bird stands close to the top of the list. There's not a sound or movement or spot of color in that high drama that I've forgotten, or will ever forget.

When I first met the Cohutta gobbler, I had no faint suspicion that he and I were embarking on such a splendid outdoor adventure. The woods were dressed in pastel shades of greens and golds and splotched with chalky clumps of dogwood, making them seem almost unreal. This was spring gobbling season in the mountains, and I was hunting alone in the Cohutta Range on the Georgia-Tennessee line.

For me, this is one of the most stimulating hunt seasons of the year. The forest floor is bright with flowers, tree buds are bursting with new life, and the vitality of the woods and its creatures make it seem on the verge of erupting into some unbelievable fantasy of sound and color.

At dawn I'd walked out the backbone of an isolated ridge and paused to listen for resonant notes that might indicate a big buck turkey on its roost or on the prowl. For an hour I stood there with my back against an oak tree, while the dawn woods came to life and the sun touched a distant mountain with burnished copper.

About flying-down time, when there's light enough for a turkey to distinguish the bushes from the bobcats, I yelped the cedar box in my hand, making notes like those of an amorous hen. This sound will sometimes set a silent old tom's genes to percolating and motivate him to reply with a lusty gobble to tell his intended that he's in the mood to solve her problem--and his.

When, after fifteen minutes, my yelps brought no response, I strolled another quarter mile along the ridgetop to try again.

There I first heard him, somewhere beyond the wild jumble of ridges and valleys sprawled out below me. His notes, high-pitched and vibrant, denoted an old gobbler. From long experience I knew that the closer I could get without spooking him, the better my chances would be to put him in the bag so I struck out in a beeline across the ragged series of ridges, navigating the rough valleys and pausing on each ridge to call and get an answer.

On the fourth ridge I sensed that he was somewhere near. When I clucked my yelper and didn't get an answer, I considered that the bird and I were at close range. I stood motionless, straining my ears, and after a few minutes heard some creature working in the dry leaves that blanketed the shallow cove just beyond the hilltop. The crest of the summit was thinly clad in laurel, and the ground around the thickets was reasonably bare of leaves. In a half-crouch to keep my head below the narrow backbone of the ridge, I circled to a point directly above where I could hear the parched leaves rattling.

After listening for a moment, I concluded definitely that the sound was made by turkeys scratching for sustenance in the brown carpet, though they hadn't made a note of any kind to verify their presence. I stood perfectly still, trying to determine what my next move should be.

I have little doubt that I'd have concocted some scheme to get a look at those birds over my gunsights, if a gray squirrel hadn't chosen that exact moment to make a trip through the scrubby timber. When I heard him rattle the bark on a tree above me, I instinctively glanced up. The squirrel was so close I could have touched him with the tip of my gun barrel. I had my camouflage clothing on but had neglected to smear my face that morning with bowhunter's paint, preferring instead to use a gauze mask when the time came to sit in a blind and call up a gobbler.

When the squirrel saw my white face and identified me, he seemed to go berserk. He made a flying arc to the next tree, another long leap, and then in his third jump he either misjudged distance or broke a limb in his headlong flight. I got a glimpse of him in midair, then heard him hit the leaves on the slope below.

If those startled turkeys had taken to the sky, I could have killed one. They were scratching within forty feet of where I stood. When I heard them running in the leaves, I charged through the laurel, hoping for a shot. But by the time I spotted the birds, they were sprinting up the far slope, out of shotgun range. One was the tallest gobbler I'd ever seen in the woods. He simply dwarfed the two jakes with him.

The season was running out, but I spent my last eight days on the trail of that big turkey. I still feel that if all those slopes were piled on top of one another, I must have climbed a hundred miles high. Joel Biggs, a local wildlife officer, told me that turkeys often range as far as four or five miles, and I must have looked in every cove and on top of every ridge in those twenty square miles.

I hunted through the open seasons in Georgia and Tennessee and on the Ocoee Wildlife Management Area. On five different occasions I could have put a young gobbler in the bag, but I passed up each one. One had a raspy voice I thought belonged to my old bird. He gave me a few hair-raising moments. Yet when he walked around the end of a log, fifty feet away, I saw that his beard was no longer than my index finger.

I was stricken with big turkey fever. That huge gobbler had my tag on him and I wanted him more than any big game trophy I'd ever brought home--and that included sheep, bears, elk, and caribou.

Before the hunt was over that spring, I met one other mountain man who was on the trail of this same bird. Gobbler hunters have a special feeling of camaraderie. If they happen to meet on a high ridge or isolated woodland trail, it's like two Daniel Boones bumping into one another. They exchange cordialities either by sign language or in whispers, briefly swap plans so they won't conflict in choice of territory, and trade bits of information on fresh scratchings or other sign. They might even take a few minutes off to compare the tones of their turkey calls. Then, for the remainder of the day, each man will listen for the sound of the other's gun--hoping all the while he won't hear it.

This grizzled mountaineer I met came down the trail as softly as a forest cat. After the usual ritual of greetings, he showed me his call and I yelped my box for him. The old fellow listened with a slightly cocked ear to the notes, then nodded.

"Gobblers around here shore oughta like that Southern accent," he commented. Since he seemed a very affable and gracious fellow, I took his words with a grain of saltpeter.

During the three seasons that I devoted my full attention to this long-bearded old patriarch of the forest, I learned all over again that killing a large wild gobbler presents perhaps the greatest challenge in hunting. It doesn't take the courage needed to coldly face a charging grizzly or the stamina necessary to climb for a mountain goat or trophy ram. But nothing else requires more in woodsmanship, patience, and ingenuity.

As I said, I stayed on the trail of the Cohutta gobbler for three seasons. I filed my license in my home state of Georgia and took birds in Alabama, Mississippi, Oklahoma, and New Mexico, and could have added Tennessee to the list with a lesser gobbler, had there not been only this one I was truly interested in.

To make the cheese more binding, as they say in Crackerese, I learned that my old gobbler had already acquired a reputation in both the Cohutta Mountains and around Ocoee. Several of the local sportsmen had an eye on him, and more than a few had devoted most of their spring gunning to the bird. So I approached each April season with the growing apprehension that one of those mountain men might get to the gobbler before I had another chance at it.

I saw the bird a number of times. It seemed to lead a charmed life. Only once could I have blown the whistle on him. He walked across the road in front of my car. He was only a few yards away when I stopped, jumped from behind the steering wheel, and threw a shell into the chamber of my gun. The huge gobbler walked unhurriedly and almost majestically up the slope, as though he knew just as well as I that I wouldn't shoot. To bushwhack that old patriarch would have been as heinous a crime as ambushing my best friend.

Once I called him to within seventy-five yards of my blind. For thirty minutes he stayed in one spot, strutting and gobbling. Then he vanished as suddenly and completely as if he had been erased. It made me wonder if I'd seen him at all and should seek psychiatric help.

On another occasion I ran into him at least a couple of miles from where we'd first met. He was on the Georgia side of the line, on the last day of the Georgia open season. I was traveling a long "lead" (which is the local term for a main ridge) just after daylight. When I paused on the brow of a slope to call, he answered. At least, I was almost certain I recognized his voice.

I made a breathless detour of more than a mile to the ridge above him. But before I could get into position, half a dozen crows spotted the tom. Ganging up on and harassing a lone wild turkey is a favorite crow pastime, and from their language I knew they were really working this one over.

I crept downhill as close as I dared to get to the melee and set up my stand for business. For more than an hour we maneuvered around on that point of the ridge. Finally the crows, or an unknown intruder, or something I said on my wingbone call or cedar box spooked him. Or maybe he just got tired of playing games. He turned away and crossed a shallow cove to the thick laurel, but when he hit the open ridgetop they found him again. Finally the whole sideshow continued out of hearing over the crest.

The foreboding that someone else would get to that gobbler before me grew acute when, on the third season of our acquaintance, I had to miss the first three open days. My only consolation was that spring came later than usual that year and those first legal days were rainy and cold, which might somewhat dampen the ardor between toms and hens, normally in full blossom by then. As for the dedicated gobbler hunters, I knew they'd be in the woods even if we were in the middle of a second ice age.

On the morning of the fourth day, I was on the mountain half an hour before daylight. The brown carpet of leaves was white with frost, and a cold blanket of air lay across the hills.

I wasn't exactly pleased with the way my plans had been disrupted on this particular morning. Phil Stone (an old hunting partner) and I had decided to hunt together through the gobbling hours, then separate and scout out a tremendous territory for signs. My wife Kayte refused to stay in camp alone and insisted on coming with us.

Three's a crowd, even at turkey hunting, so when we parked in a little gap, Phil took off down a dim logging road that skirted a narrow valley. I'd have sent Kayte in the other direction, but she gets lost even in our backyard, and I knew we'd then have to spend the rest of the season looking for her. So she stayed with me, which meant confining my hunting to the more gentle terrain around the car.

As the first dawn light turned the woods from black to gray, a ruffed grouse flashed across the road. Farther down the valley we flushed two more of these colorful birds out of a branch bottom. The dawn was bright and cold as we climbed the point of a low ridge overlooking the valley. From this spot I knew we were high enough to hear turkeys on any of the half dozen ridges sloping away from that massive range around Big Frog Mountain. Kayte and I got settled and waited until the noise we'd made in the frozen leaves was forgotten by the forest creatures around us and they began to move about once more.

On my box I gave the low, plaintive notes of a hen. After a few minutes without an answer, I called much louder. A quarter of an hour later, I rattled the box with the throaty call of a gobbler. All this activity produced exactly no results, except for the raucous notes of a crow across the valley and the loud drumming of a woodpecker on a hollow stub nearby.

Kayte and I climbed over the crest of the ridge into the next valley to repeat our performance. The sun spotlighted the tops of the highest hills and the line of light gradually crept down the mountains until it touched and warmed our half-numb hands and cheeks.

We moved from one ridge to another and heard nothing that resembled the notes of a turkey. At 8:30 A.M. we made our way back over the trail to where we met Phil Stone, who'd also gone through an unproductive session.

The three of us discussed the situation and decided that, with the season so retarded, the birds were not yet courting and probably not even speaking to one another. This evaluation gave me a vast sense of relief, along with some assurance that my big gobbler had not yet been disturbed and that I'd see him again somewhere in these mountain woods.

Kayte and Phil were already in the car, impatiently waiting for me while licking their chops in anticipation over the Bloody Marys they would soon be having at breakfast. I don't know whether it was impulse, instinct, or some strange intuition that suddenly impelled me to step away from the car to the edge of the road with the turkey call in my hand.

I clucked a couple of times, gave the low, breathless notes of a hen, and then listened. No response. I'd expected none. Still, merely to complete the routine, I halfheartedly rattled my box to simulate the call of a gobbler.

There was nothing halfhearted in the challenge that bounced back from the next ridge, almost quickly enough to pass for an echo.

I have no idea how my two partners got out of the car and beside me so fast and so noiselessly, but they now appeared to have lost all interest in breakfast and Bloody Marys. I touched my finger to my lips.

"Stand here a few minutes," I whispered, "and let's see which direction he's headed."

When the buck turkey gobbled again, he was a hundred yards farther down the ridge. That was enough for me. My partners agreed that I could travel faster and get ahead of the gobbler if I went alone, and that I also might have a better chance of seeing and definitely identifying him as the one bird I wanted. As for myself, I already knew.

I climbed the slope then circled the side of the hill in a half-run. At the spot where I hoped to intercept the gobbler, I zipped up my camouflage suit and sat down at the base of a big tree with emerald vegetation growing before it.

I wasn't sure yet who it was the tom answered, but he gobbled again shortly after I'd given him the soft, gentle notes of a hen on my slate-type call. Minutes later a second gobbler, this one with a younger voice, set the woods to ringing off to my left.

The smaller tom definitely was coming to me, but the turkey I had planned to intercept walked off his ridge, crossed a rivulet in the hollow, and climbed to a cove that angled away from where I'd taken my stand.

I left the young buck turkey decoying to my squeal and took off across the slope. I didn't even try to convince myself I was acting foolishly in giving up a bird in the hand for a try at that old boy with the rusty pipes. The big tom had already cost me at least five gobblers since I'd first met him. I figured he should be worth at least one more.

By midmorning the leaves had lost their frosty coating. The drying forest floor became much noisier underfoot. I had to pause every few minutes to get another fix on the gobbler, who continued to answer my calls. We were walking at about the same speed. By the time I reached the road that separated Georgia's Cohutta Range from Tennessee's Ocoee, the tom had crossed the road and climbed the side of a massive mountain into the forbidden area.

This appeared to be the end of the trail. The Ocoee area was closed except for five two-day periods in April, and I wouldn't have another chance at him until then. It looked like old long-beard had once again given me the shaft.

By all sane criteria, I knew it was hardly possible to entice that cagey gobbler to backtrack so late in the day over the route he'd just taken. Especially since he had been intent on going the other way from the moment we'd first heard him.

One thing for sure. I had nothing to lose by trying. I whacked my cedar box with a couple of lusty yelps. Almost instantly, he came back with a high-pitched gobble. I settled down in a little clump of pines in legal territory to wait. At least ten minutes went by before his resonant tones again rolled down the mountain--and this time they seemed to come from farther off. I waited. His next call came from near the top of the mountain. There wasn't any doubt in my mind now that he was walking out of the picture. In desperation I gobbled my box as loud as I could make it quaver.

For a full twenty minutes, complete silence. Then he sounded off again from approximately the same spot where I'd last heard him. My heart gave an extra thump or two. At least I'd stopped his flight ... momentarily.

I waited. And waited. And waited. I have no idea how long I sat in that one spot, trying to convince myself he'd already gone on and over the mountain. I suppose the only thing that kept the seat of my pants pressed against the unfriendly rocks and roots was the knowledge that many times when a tom stops gobbling, but hasn't been spooked, he's coming to investigate. If so, there wasn't any harm in giving him my exact location. Stealthily I reached for the slate and cedar stick, touched them softly together for a few dainty clucks, then dropped them beside me on the ground. Most novice hunters are likely to call much too much.

To wait--and keep on waiting--requires an enormous amount of patience. Even more so, when there's no hint of any kind whether you are on the verge of success.

At last I gave up. The rocks and roots now seemed to be actively attacking my hindquarters. My legs felt numb from sitting in one position. Phil and Kayte--and beyond them the Bloody Marys, country sausage, eggs, and biscuits--were waiting. I hadn't heard a peep out of my gobbler for three-quarters of an hour. By now he could be in the next county. With disappointment welling through me, I shifted my position to reach for the slate and cedar stick I had dropped to the ground.

Suddenly somewhere a limb or twig cracked, the sound a deer makes as it tiptoes through the woods. I came to full attention again, straining my eyes for a glimpse of feet or head or brown deerhide. For a dozen minutes I sat motionless. At last I decided that the animal or whatever that had cracked that stick must have drifted on by.

Once more I relaxed and prepared to gather up my gear and call it a day. I was on the verge of standing up to give my numb muscles some relief when I heard footsteps in the leaves. The cadence was exactly that of a man who slips stealthily along, stalking unseen quarry.

Again I froze. I couldn't see a man or make out movement of any kind, but at that moment there wasn't anything I needed less than a load of high brass No. 4 or 6 pellets smack in my face.

I had been straining so hard to see some deer or human form that my first glimpse of the gobbler now came as a distinct shock. He was beyond and walking parallel to a contour that dropped off like a terrace about twenty yards in front of my blind. The contour hid all but the meaty wrinkled top of his head above the wattles. I couldn't see enough yet to definitely identify him as the old patriarch who had led me on a merry three-year chase, but that one glimpse still had me all shook up inside.

He took two more steps, bringing his head higher up above the contour, but I still couldn't see his beard or judge his size. He put his head down to peck at something on the forest floor, and while his eye was out of sight I quickly raised my gun. On its way up, the gun dislodged in a dead Y-shaped stem. It straddled and lodged on the gun barrel in such a way that I couldn't see the sights. The bird continued to walk, growing taller and taller as it came up the shoulder of the hill, and I moved the barrel slowly to keep it in line with his head.

It was purely a matter of luck that at the same moment my gobbler walked behind a large tree trunk, a protruding twig suddenly flipped the Y-stem from my barrel. When the tom stepped past the tree, my sights were directly on his head.

My 12-gauge Winchester pump was loaded with shells holding No. 6 shot. Some hunters like large shot--No. 4 or No. 2--but I know I have a better chance of hitting the vital parts of a bird's head and neck with a denser pattern. Most shots in this type of hunting are at a bird's head and neck while he's still on the ground. I often back up my first round of No. 6 with a No. 4 and then a No. 2 load, which gives me a reserve of progressively larger pellets to break down a turkey that flies or runs after the first shot.

There he stood for all of five seconds with his head up in a patch of sunlight, as tall and majestic as I remembered him from two springs with my gun. The sunlight on his feathers made them ripple in a display of copper, green, and gold so resplendent that I caught my breath. What a beauty. Then I saw his heavy beard and knew beyond any doubt that he was indeed the old patriarch I'd dreamed about for so long.

It was almost sacrilegious to shatter that magnificent moment with a shot--but the powerful impulses developed in a lifetime of hunting triggered the gun. It was a clean, one-shot kill.

That's when all the excitement of the past two hours finally hit me. My hands shook as I tried to unstrap the camera from my shoulder. When I hefted the bird for weight and saw how far I had to lift his feet so that his head would clear the ground, I got the shakes all over again.

He pulled the hand on the corroded old camp scales up to twenty five and a half pounds--the largest mountain gobbler I've seen, and one of the biggest turkeys I had ever killed, including the heavier breeds from some of the Southern plantations.

Phil peered wonderingly over his glasses at the scales.

"There just ain't no telling," he said, "what this critter might have weighed, if these scales weren't so rusty." (We checked them later on and found that the scales did, in fact, read almost one and a half pounds too low.)

At that moment though, the gobbler's weight didn't make too much difference. He had given me my finest hunt in turkey woods, and he still remains my most highly prized big game trophy.

2

GYPSY

By Jerry Gibbs

Outdoor Life, December 1979

The death of a beloved gun dog and friend takes a terrible toll on a hunter. If the dog is also a member of the family, the sadness and grief is even worse. My good friend Jerry Gibbs, however, had to endure pain that few bird-dog men will ever have to experience and this is fortunate. Jerry could not write this story for many years and when you read this true heart-wrenching story, you will know the reason.

A black dog came into our lives a while ago. She was a seal-shiny, big-footed pup, unable from the time she could walk to ignore the call of a nose that promised the best of life's wind-borne mysteries. She was a wanderer. Because of that, we named her Gypsy.

Gypsy was a Labrador retriever. Books and trainers acclaim the versatility of the breed, and versatility was what I thought I needed when we decided it was time to get a dog. Later I learned not to rely on textbook generalities. They sometimes lead to trouble, even tragedy. And I learned about something else you can't take literally: a dog owner's declaration that the heartache of losing a beloved animal is too much to face again. "No more dogs, not ever," he might say. Don't believe it. If you love dogs, you won't want to be without one, regardless of what may come. But let me tell you about Gypsy.

I had been a long time without a dog. My wife, Judy, and I had lived some time in suburban apartments, but when we had a couple of boys we needed a house. To me, the best thing about the increased space was that there was room for a dog. We were barely moved in when we found her.

We built a soft nest in a washtub for carrying the pup home from the breeder. She easily convinced our older son, Greg, then six, that other places were better. A knot near the tip of her tail gave the appendage the appearance of a windblown flag. That slightly canted tail beat merrily as she wormed herself from the tub onto Greg's lap. She was asleep in moments.

A dog becomes a physical part of your life immediately. Emotionally, it just takes a little longer.

You rarely remember the inconveniences of raising a pup. It's the way you remember kids growing up, the good parts stick. With a dog it's the funny, crazy times, and the way the animal earns your admiration and respect if it's any good at all as a hunter.

Gypsy was a water dog. She was seven weeks old when we got her. A week later she traveled with us on a camping trip to Cape Hatteras, North Carolina. She was too young for water training; in fact I had yet to introduce her to any water deeper than her drinking pail. It didn't matter. She bounced down the beach, a coal-black India-rubber ball, then looked up and suddenly discovered the ocean. With her four feet planted defiantly in the sand, she eyed the wind-lashed surf, barked several times, and waded into the wash. Throughout the trip, she galloped in the shallows, chased herring gulls and sandpipers, and dug caverns in the sand. I started her formal training soon after we returned home.

The intensity and single-mindedness of a retriever bent on capturing a dummy or a bird is special, a beautiful thing. Gypsy was barely able to mouth the smallest training dummy I could find, but she managed with no coaxing. I remember how she grew into the dummies. My memory of her is like an elapsed-time-sequence film. I see her growing from bouncing puppy to sleek retrieving machine, her chest in an air-borne arc ending in that explosive, flat-out water entry unique to retrievers. Gypsy had spirit and desire; she needed only refining and control.

As Gypsy's training continued, one thing bothered me. Occasionally she broke from a retrieve to follow some intriguing scent. Other times, she seemed to hit a scent and to turn deaf to return commands, running through backyards and down suburban roads. I tried the usual remedies, from check cords to discipline. They seemed to work for a while. Friends experienced in dog training chalked up the dog's weakness either to my inept training or to some flaw in her makeup.

The problem did not appear consistently. Long stretches of perfect behavior tended to make us forget Gypsy's occasional lapses. Besides, she was an inseparable member of the family. There were hilarious times when Judy or I released Gypsy into the midst of our boys' softball games. The dog knew exactly what was going on. She charged into the field, seized the ball, and ran the bases several times before stopping. If she went after a just-hit ball, she frequently clipped the base runner, bowling him over for a certain out, then licked his face despite howls of protest.

Gypsy loved winter. She chased our boys' toboggans and usually leaped aboard just before the sled caromed off a mogul and sent her sailing through the air. She helped our younger boy, Jon, learn to cope with interference when he was trying to learn ice hockey. She played husky in a harness while towing provisions lashed on a sled to winter camp. But it was water that Gypsy loved most of all.

After she began to work heavily on water retrieves, Gypsy rarely allowed the boys to swim in peace. The dog would swim around them, grabbing T-shirts. Much to his annoyance, Jon was retrieved more than once. As author James Michener once wrote, a Lab is "a kind of perpetual five-year-old, forever young, forever loving."

Gypsy was rarely content to rest. With typical retriever hardiness, she broke through thin ice to complete a retrieve. If I thought conditions were perhaps a bit dangerous and therefore threw nothing, she crashed in anyway, then clambered ashore like a bear, showering pinwheels of frigid water on spectators.

None of her breaking and running problems were apparent during water work. She quickly learned to retrieve among decoys without becoming entangled in their anchor cords. I was amazed at the speed with which she learned to make multiple retrieves, to take a line on hand signals, and even to check on command in the midst of one retrieve and head for another target. I shouldn't have been surprised, for the miracle of retrievers is their incredible memory and intelligence. On land, though, Gypsy's problem continued to recur periodically.

I began to hear of others whose dogs had similar problems. One fellow from Iowa had spent a considerable sum on professional training in hopes that his high-spirited Lab could be used for flushing pheasants, as so many are. The trainer had accomplished some things but made no guarantees. The dog's owner had several good days, but eventually the dog locked in on one bird that either was running or had left a scent too strong to resist. The big male Lab cannonballed through the cornfields out of sight. Eventually the owner brought him back with the whistle, but, from then on, the dog was totally unreliable as a controlled flusher. Another chap in Nebraska had the same experience. At heel, sometimes on a check thong, his Lab functioned as a retriever after pointing dogs locked in and the gunners brought the raucous cock pheasants down. I didn't like the sound of any of it and went back to preparing Gypsy for waterfowl hunting.

Gypsy's first birds were ducks--big orange-leg blacks and fat greenhead mallards from the salt marshes of southern New Jersey. Here, hip-deep black-gumbo muck awaits the returning hunter who has neglected to pull his boat up on the marsh at high tide. But the birds are there on the creeks or far back in the potholes where few hunters care to slog. We had some good days, that Gypsy dog and I, and I'll remember every one of them. Sometimes we lay flat on the far edges of marsh, away from other hunters, and waited for the birds to come. Flocks of little greenwing teal flashed in the low sun, making quick course changes as they came in. Bigger ducks would make one pass, then bore in straight. If we were lucky, they sat hard with the decoys I had packed on my back.

We had skies full of Canada and snow geese to watch, and silly grebes to laugh at as we motored back up the big creek. We savored the raspy cry of a startled great blue heron, and that special kind of tiredness that comes after a day of work that you truly love.

Once, during a rain, I explored a section of marsh where I had never been. It was a high marsh, the grasses taller than my head.

Gypsy and I pushed far back, though the going was tough and became tougher. Small holes pocked the marsh. From time to time, we put up a duck. So intriguing was this country that I forgot the reason for the height of the grasses--tide.

When I realized that water was deepening around my boots, I stepped on a small hummock, made a reconnaissance of our position, and began to worry. We had paralleled the side of the marsh from which the flood tide now came. I could not retrace my steps before the water would become too deep and I could not cut out of the marsh as I had planned. I had to move inland. I was tired, but there was no choice.

As we moved ahead, the marsh became softer. With each step I sank calf deep, then knee deep in muck. Rain came in sheets, smoking across the seemingly endless marsh, obliterating the grassy plain before us. I was as wet from perspiration as I would have been without my waterproof parka.

Ducks flushed from potholes in front of us, almost close enough to touch, but I had no time or interest for them. I had to will each step now. My breathing was ragged. Still the tide pressed from behind. I knelt a moment to rest. Gypsy must have understood the seriousness of the situation because she walked close to me. When I faltered, she bumped me with the solid 75 pounds. At first I was enraged; then I realized what she was doing.

We went on like that for what seemed hours before the footing gradually firmed. I staggered in the rain back to the camper, drank two quarts of water, stripped, and began to dry off. Gypsy curled on her pad, steaming, smelling like wet dog and looking at me with an expression that seemed to say, "Really, we weren't in all that much trouble." I was exhausted. I lay in my bunk wondering just how much she really had contributed to getting me back. Even after all of that, I could not accept the dog's faulty behavior on land.

I persisted in trying to work her in upland covers. At times she worked to perfection, quartering ahead, working field or woodland edge in classic form. Then she took interest in something and drifted away. There was no consistency.

I began working her at heel while walking up birds. She bolted very few times during this training. Unhappily, I realized this might be the only way I could trust her away from water. Not long afterward, we moved to northern Vermont.

Big lakes, freshwater swamps, and potholes promised new waterfowling opportunities. We lived in a cottage on a large lake. A decaying blind stood within an easy walk. From it Gypsy retrieved her first north-country black duck. Whistlers, buffleheads, geese, and mergansers used the big water. Greg was old enough to join me that first season. He held the dog while I broke the clear skim ice so we could set the decoys in the predawn darkness.

The second season the boy helped me construct a blind on the far side of the lake. We hauled lumber and drove corner stakes while Gypsy swam from shore to blind, explored the beach, and watched our work. She seemed more content to stay close than I had ever seen her. Maybe it was the newness of it all, maybe something else. Those warm, late-summer days of blind building and hauling out decoys are some of the finest in memory. Greg and I watched as the dog swam and ran the beach.

The grouse cycle started up again in Vermont. Back in old, rough highland pastures and abandoned orchards, we flushed more birds than I had seen in a long time. In spring the drummers had thumped like old generators. The broods had come through that worrisome period, and now we were finding not only singles but coveys of young ruffed grouse yet to split up. The hunting was impossible to resist.

I made a couple of successful hunts alone, holding Gypsy by command at heel. Grouse hunting looked good, and it was time to start Greg on these wonderful birds. One afternoon we hunted near the house that we'd built far back on an old logging road. We walked down that road, then cut into the broken woodland. This was mostly thick cover, and any shooting would be fast. I gave the boy the left-handed position. If the going became too rough or too confusing, he could cut to the roadside to get his bearings. To be safe, we talked or whistled back and forth constantly as we moved ahead, revealing our positions.

Gypsy was at a tight heel, anxious for a shot bird and the retrieve. Shortly, two birds exploded in front of Greg. When I asked why he didn't shoot, he said he couldn't believe how fast they went. We laughed and moved ahead. Another bird rocketed off somewhere between us, closer to me, but too far to my left for a safe shot. I let it go. Greg had dropped a little behind, and while I told him to move up, a bird thundered through the trees off my right shoulder. Evidently it had been sitting in a tree, and it had let me pass as grouse sometimes do. The bird flew somewhat toward me, then made a 90-degree turn going away. I fired once and missed. As I began lowering the 20-gauge, another grouse burst from the ground in dense cover just ahead and slightly to the right. I wheeled quickly and locked in on its low flight. As I began to pull the trigger, my brain screamed a warning to stop. Peripheral vision detected a black, blurred shape bolting at the bird, but the message was an instant too late. The primer was punched and the shot on its way before my responses caught up, and I pulled the barrels up in a hopeless attempt to correct. I remember the roar of my voice over the sound of the gun, then a scream of pain. The dog wheeled in circles as I ran to her and dropped to my knees. I cradled her in my arms, seeing where some of the shot had cut through the top of her back. I tried to console her, tried. ...

Gypsy had stopped crying by the time Greg reached us. Her breathing was ragged, but she did not cry. Her head was on my arm. She watched me patiently, fully trusting me to make things well again. Through blurred eyes I saw that Greg had moved swiftly; no man could have reacted better in an emergency. Both guns were broken, the shells were shucked, and he asked whether I needed help to carry her out. I sent him to bring his mother with the truck. I worked my arms gently beneath the dog, lifted her, and stumbled to the road.

"She'll be all right, won't she?" Greg pleaded. I had nothing to tell him.

The scene of moments before ran over and over in my mind. Never cured of her tendency to break, Gypsy had bolted while I turned away to fire at the first bird. She must have nearly caught the second bird as it frantically beat through the thick, low cover. She had leaped after the escaping grouse into my line of fire.

"Let's hope no pellet struck the spinal column," the veterinarian said. "If it did--well, she could be paralyzed--or she just might not make it. I won't encourage you, or take away all hope."

While the doctor gave her several injections, she watched me quietly, patiently, and with trust. I put a hand beneath her head. She took one deep breath, then rested. I knew she would not live.

Gypsy died during the night. I buried her near a group of birches on a flat place overlooking the woods, the valley below and the lake, where the duck blind went unused that season. If there is any kind of justice, I know where she is right now. There is a shore with an endless beach to run, a sky full of ducks, and a kid or two to throw sticks and swim with her. Hie on, Gypsy. There's nothing to stop you now.

3

THE INVINCIBLE GROUSE HUNTER

By Joel M. Vance

You'll remember this story next time you pass an abandoned farmhouse or deserted cabin, especially if night is approaching and you're having a little unexpected trouble finding your way to the road where you parked your car. When the landmarks vanish and suddenly everything looks unfamiliar, perhaps even supernatural, just keep in mind that nothing in the woods really wants to harm you. And if you chance to encounter a spectral old man on a rickety porch, just rocking in silence as he hungers for one more hunt, there's no cause to be alarmed. Of course, it would be wise to be respectful and to assure him you wouldn't knowingly hunt his land without permission. Explain your predicament to him and maybe--just maybe--he'll befriend you.

Is this really fiction? Joel Vance won't say.

I don't know where I made the wrong turn. It was a dark day, with scudding clouds, flat-lit, chill and damp, and there are few landmarks in the North Country. The spruces huddled defensively, as if expecting hard times, and the birch and aspen waved white, ineffectual arms at the snapping November wind.

But grouse season is grouse season, and mean weather is no reason to stay home, so Chip and I pressed on through the deep woods, the dog following his red nose, me following the dog.

Maybe the first grouse flush is where I went wrong. It was one of those birds that jump just after you've passed, giving you at best an awkward twisting shot to the left. I can't remember ever hitting a bird like that, and I didn't then--missed it clean but shot off a couple of innocent birch sprouts. I cussed the bird admiringly, without heat, and watched him set his wings and sail over the next sand-and-granite ridge, through the leafless birches. I figured I had him pretty well marked, so I called in Chip and we slogged that way.

Then a second bird went up without warning. I missed that one, too. No one ever accused me of threatening the local grouse population. I knew I had this one spotted--saw it land and run a few feet. So I eagerly abandoned the first bird and trotted after the second one. I vaguely remember skirting the springy edge of a bog, then pushing my way through head-high clumps of alder, but I killed the bird on the rise and added a woodcock at what I took to be the far edge of the thicket.

Only, when I tried to retrace my path, nothing looked familiar. That's the way the North Country is, featureless, thick with trees and broken only by potholes where deer water and beavers swim. They always know where they are or, if they don't, they really don't care. I cared. I was thoroughly lost and it was afternoon and I really didn't want to spend a cold night in the woods.

Normally I wear a pocket compass, a little clip-on job that I can use to find magnetic north. Naturally, it was clipped to my other shirt, the red one I wear when I'm hunting with someone else. The one at home in the closet.

"Damn," I said aloud. I called Chip in and sat on a moss-covered log to think about it. "We're lost, friend," I said. "Lost in big country...."

He leaned against me and I admired his simple (and probably misplaced) trust. He'd follow me to hell and beyond, certain that I'd provide. I tried to retrace my route mentally, but of course I couldn't be certain of anything. Still, any decision was better than no decision at all, so I chose a line of travel and picked a distant spruce tip as a reference point. If only the damned sun would come out! But the day remained gray, shrouded and sullen.

I made a couple of detours around bogs in the next hour, and once toured the shore of a small lake, for few North Country lakes these days are without an access road. But this was one of the exceptions.

And then I did stumble onto a road. Literally, for I stepped onto a carpet of ferns, went down through them, and saved myself from tumbling headlong onto the roadbed only by an ungraceful, stumbling recovery. It certainly was no heavily used trail, and the sand was undisturbed and largely grown over with invading plants. A couple of wind-downed trees bore mute testimony that no one, at least in a vehicle, had passed this way for a long time. Perhaps it was an old logging trail. But it had to come from somewhere and go somewhere, so I picked the left for no reason and started that way.

It must have been a mile or more later that I rounded a bend in the rutted trail and spied the house. There was far less light now, though when I checked my watch it was only mid-afternoon. It certainly was not late enough to account for the perceptible dimming. No, the day seemed overhung by an unnatural darkness. It was as if I were being hovered over by something large and ominous, and when that occurred to me I looked up instinctively, then laughed at my quick, irrational fear. Panic at being lost.

The house looked uninhabited. It certainly had not been painted for a long time. It was tall and spare, a typical North Country farmhouse with tall window-frames, clapboard siding, a galvanized roof now gone to rust, lightning arresters, a sagging porch. The house was as gray as the sky. Even though I was certain no one lived there, I circled the building, kicking through the matted weeds. I peered in through a couple of windows, but they were so clouded over that I couldn't see inside. Then, as I returned to the front porch, I started in quick fear, for there was a man sitting in an old rocker on the porch.

"Jeez! You startled me!" I exclaimed, my heart thumping. The man didn't move. He was in shadow, not at all distinct. He said nothing. "I'm sorry for prowling around," I said, embarrassed. "I didn't see you sitting there." I moved up on the first of the two steps to the porch and got a better look at him.

He sat very straight in the battered rocker, his strong, ridged and knobbed old hands on his knees. He wore a battered felt hat, a faded checkered flannel shirt, red-and-yellow vertical-striped suspenders, and gray pants with leather facing on the thighs.

"Partridge hunting?" he asked in a whispery voice as dry as the rustle of mousefeet.

I nodded. "I got lost. I wasn't hunting on your place. Don't want you to think I'd hunt without permission."

"Asking's right," he said. "I like that." His voice was more than just old. It was as if it came from a long, long way off. "I don't care if you do hunt here," he said. "Right good for partridge, too. There's a covey of four or five down there in that alder swamp."

"Well, I really ought to be getting on home," I said. "Except I don't know where home is. Don't know where I am now, either."

"You're here," the old man said. "And that's good enough, ain't it?" He paused for a moment while I tried to think of an answer, then went on. "Ain't many people find their way back in here. Them that do I show something special."

I began to wonder if the old man wasn't more than a little cracked. The whole situation puzzled me--an apparently deserted house, the sudden appearance of the motionless oldtimer--even the atmosphere seemed charged with eerie energy. Chip whined and nuzzled at my hand. Usually he was all bark and bustle around strangers.

"There's an old road about half a quarter through that pine grove," said the old man, as if sensing my unease. "Take a right and go about a mile and you'll hit the county highway." I relaxed. He was just a harmless old coot, cabin-feverish maybe, but nothing to spook at.

"Fore you leave, though, why don't you go down and hunt up that swamp covey. I'd kind of like to see somebody put them up, just one more time."

It was a kind offer, and I guessed maybe he was crippled to the point where he couldn't hunt and just liked to sit and enjoy a vicarious hunt. "Nice gun you're carryin'," he said. "Smith, ain't it?"

"Wouldn't shoot anything but an old double," I said. "There's something about these old side-bys."

"Ever seen one like this?" he asked, and for the first time I saw a gun leaning against the porch railing near him. And such a gun!

It was the most beautiful shotgun I'd ever seen. Every part of the receiver was intricately whorled with engraving. The trigger guard held sinuous designs, the locking lever glowed with finely chiseled patterns. The lovely figured stock had such a deep finish it was like looking into a dark woods pool. "My God!" I breathed reverently, "That's the most beautiful shotgun I've ever seen!" "Right pretty," agreed the old man. "Ain't been used for quite a while. I'd like to see her work one more time. Why don't you take her down to the alders and see if you can put up a bird?" "Oh, no--I couldn't!" I protested, though of course I wanted desperately to pick up that lovely shotgun, caress it, admire it, shoulder it, and hear it chant ancient thunder at flying birds.

The old man turned his head slightly and his eyes caught mine and it was as if I were being pulled toward him. I took a step and picked up the gun. Other than the slight turn of his head, the old man hadn't moved, hands still on his knees, curiously white for an outdoorsman. For just an instant I looked deep into his faded blue eyes and saw--what? Darkness, perhaps, and infinite sadness and, I think, cold worlds spinning through eternity. I inhaled sharply with unaccountable fear; then the old man looked down the hill at the alder thicket. "Would you take my old dog along?" he asked. "She's gettin' on, but she's game for a short hunt."

I hadn't seen any dog, but he whistled faintly and an arthritic old setter limped out of the shadows in the yard, looking toward the porch. "You'll just about have time to hunt the alders and make it out to your road before dark," the old man said. "Let me see Dolly work before the dark comes."

I looked at the wondrous shotgun. It was a Parker, legendary for that reason if for no other, but finer by far than any of the admittedly few Parkers I'd ever seen. "Go on, now," whispered the old man, his voice a gentle shove that guided me off the porch. Chip heeled tight to my leg, his ears laid back, whining softly. But Dolly moved stiffly down the hill toward the thicket and it was his dog the old man wanted to see, not mine, so I let Chip trail me.

I examined the gun more closely, and noticed the serial number-- 200,001--on the trigger guard tang. Also inlaid in fine gold were the initials Wm.P. How could some old woods rat ever have come by a shotgun as obviously valuable as this one? I decided to talk with the sheriff--but not until I got a chance to use it on those alder-swamp birds. I dropped two 12-gauge shells into the chambers with a musical "poonk!" The old dog slewed to a stop, nose full of bird smell, feathery tail a-quiver. Sure enough, the stylish point was just at the edge of the alder thicket, and I eased in behind the rigid dog, talking softly: "Easy, old girl...easy now..."

A pair of grouse flushed, one low and veering to the left, the other reaching for sky above the scrubby trees. The magic gun rose instantly to my shoulder, stock smooth as butter on my cheek. I touched the front trigger, only dimly aware of the buck of the gun, watched the bird shed feathers and its life. I tracked to the second bird in the blink of an eye and killed it cleanly at the top of the trees. No shooter I, it was the first double for me ever on grouse, and I breathed pure joy for a moment. Chip had marked the birds down and brought them to me, warm, soft and limp, one at a time. Dolly had disappeared. I smoothed the ruffs, spread the fans to admire them, and stowed the two birds in my game pocket.

"You sure had those birds nailed!" I exclaimed back at the porch. The old man had not moved. He sat now in deep shadow, his face hidden by the somber veil cast by the porch roof. I lay the birds side by side on the stoop. "Please," I said, "I'd like to leave them for you. They're yours."

"You take them," he said in a near-whisper, as if he were fading with the waning day. "I've had my share."

"Can't I do something to repay your hospitality?"

"You did it," he said. I tried to think of something to say. "Road you want is out through the pine grove."

"I should do something for you..." I faltered, for some reason anxious not to lose contact with him.

"Better be going or it'll be dark," he said, his voice dry leaves rustling in an old attic. He was almost hidden by the shadows.

"Well...what's your name?" I asked.

"Bill," he said faintly. "Just call me Bill."

Bill? William? Wm.? Maybe it was his gun, after all. There was a long silence, and I realized that if I didn't get going I would be trapped by night. I leaned the lovely shotgun against the porch railing, took one long, last look at it. "Thank you," I said. I picked up the Smith, and Chip and I started toward the pine grove.

It was dark among the tall old trees, parklike because there was no understory. I almost fell over the canted old headstone. Just a single grave marker on a long-neglected grave, heavily blanketed with fallen pine needles. I bent to read the inscription, and a chill skittered down my spine.

"William Parsons (1855-1932)
May Heaven Reward Him With A Parker,
A Good Dog, And A Plenty of Partridge"

"You're going to have to lay off the cheap booze," said my gun-fancier friend the next day when I described the gun with the serial number 200,001. "You ever hear of the Parker Invincible?"

I said I hadn't.

"There were two known," he said. "One was numbered 200,329 and the other 200,000. No one knows where 200,000 is today. There never was a 200,001." He saw the beginning of my stubborn look and raised his hands. "All I know is what I read in the records, okay?"

But as I walked back out to my car, he couldn't resist scoffing, "Remember, lay off the rotgut!"

Naturally, I went back out to the old house. And found just what I expected to find--an old, abandoned farmhouse, sagging into the years, painted inside with a thick coat of dust that was tracked only by mice and squirrels. There was no rocker on the front porch, no arthritic old setter, and no Parker Invincible, either.

I eased through the rooms, opened the closets, even climbed to the loft and peered around. Nothing. Sneezing from the dust, I went back outside. It was a bright, sunny day, and a cardinal whickered brassily from the pine grove.

A shaft of sunlight slanted through the lofty pines and splashed on the face of the tilted headstone.

Carefully, I brushed away the pine duff in front of the stone and arranged the two red 12-gauge hulls there, a memorial bouquet for a grouse hunter.

It was the least I could do for an old friend.

4

THE ULTIMATE GAMEBIRD

By Tom Huggler

*When Tom Huggler first told me about the Himalayan snowcock,
I must confess that I thought he was going to tell me a joke. But this
unique new game bird came to the United States in the 1960s and
1970s. The snowcock is a native of Central Asia and a damn tough
bird. If you think it's another easy bird to hunt, remember this: You
will only find it in the Ruby Mountains of Nevada at 10,000 feet and
you will only find one bird every square mile. Any takers?*

P icture a mountain range with craggy spires towering atop
vertical columns of stone. Imagine the peaks are split here
and there with huge fissures, and the valleys and canyons
plunge dizzily down 1,000 yards and more. Enormous
talus slides wander down the mountain's backbone. Locate
the range in Nevada. Call it the Ruby Mountains.

I first saw these rugged peaks a few years ago while a winter
sunset fired them in an afterglow of blood-red--hence, their name.
All day I had been hunting wild chukar in the nearby Humboldt
Mountains with veteran guide Bill Gibson. My legs ached from
tacking across mile-high, heart-attack hills. But I was happy, having
bagged a limit. We were taking in the sunset and resting beside
Gibson's old Suburban, whose tired engine wheezed at idle like a
panting dog.

"Someday you'll have to come back and hunt snowcocks with us. They live up there on the peaks," Gibson said, pointing to the Rubies.

"Snowcocks?"

"They're the ultimate gamebird," he continued. "A huge partridge that weighs five or six pounds, but they're incredibly wary and almost impossible to kill. They fly faster than chukar, and only a few have been taken by hunters here in Nevada."

Over a period of 30 years my love of bird hunting has taken me all over North America and even to Europe. Since collecting all of the native species of grouse and quail, I've been concentrating lately on exotic birds, and my home is beginning to look like a museum of natural history. Knowing little about snowcocks, I was determined to learn more and to some day collect one. That opportunity came in September 1991, when I joined Gibson on the last of three guided snowcock hunts that he makes each fall.

The hunting party consisted of myself and four avid sportsmen from Reno. George Kent, a retired Chevron executive, had hunted with Gibson the year before but had yet to kill a snowcock. Harry Huneycutt had moved to Nevada from Virginia 20 years ago to begin a medical practice. A sheep hunter, this was Huneycutt's first crack at these birds.

The other pair, veterinarian Andy Burnett and Bob Lawson, a school curriculum coordinator, had hired Gibson to guide them because six years of hunting on their own had produced only one snowcock.

Gibson, along with his partner, Todd White, limits most hunts to four clients. The guides only expect 50 percent success. Each of the first two hunts that fall had produced three snowcocks, although snow, hail and rain had nearly spoiled the second outing.

Now, later in the month, we had an even greater chance for bad weather. Deep snow can shut out opportunities altogether because unlike most high-country game, snowcocks don't migrate down the mountain. They scrabble out an existence on bonsai-like plants and grasses that grow along slopes and peaks bared by the winter wind. My goal was to see a snowcock and hopefully have a fair chance to shoot one.

The bird is called the snow partridge, ram chukar or snow pheasant, but its real name is the Himalayan snowcock (*Tetraogallus himalayensis*). It is one of five species of snowcocks from the high mountain ranges of central Asia.

The Himalayan snowcock occupies the Hindu Kush, Karakoram, Himalayas, Pamirs and other mountain ranges of Pakistan, Afghanistan, India and China. In the summer, shepherds and shikaris (local hunters) have seen them at altitudes nearing 20,000 feet. To elude human predators as well as eagles, vultures, jackals and even the rare snow leopard, snowcocks post sentinels and rely on keen eyesight and strong wings.

An overall gray-white in color, adult birds sport a snow-white mantle, sometimes with a hint of light blue. Snowcocks blend perfectly with their habitat and are nearly impossible to see when they freeze in position. The sexes are similar, except that males are larger in size, have more black markings about the neck and sport bumps where spurs would be expected.

The birds came to the United States through the effort of Hamilton McCaughey, a Reno sportsman who traveled to the province of Hunza, Pakistan, in 1961 to hunt Marco Polo sheep. Enamored of the Himalayan snowcock, McCaughey obtained three pairs of captured birds and carried them by porter, pony, jeep and airplane more than halfway around the world. Only one bird survived the monthlong trek, but Nevada Game Commission officials were so impressed with it and McCaughey's zeal that they decided to let him intercede on their behalf and obtain more stock from Pakistan. Nevada had 75,000 square miles of habitat devoid of gamebirds, and the snowcock seemed a likely candidate for introduction.

McCaughey arranged for a shipment of 35 more birds, 19 of which survived and were released in the Ruby Mountains in the spring of 1963. But those snowcocks disappeared. The wildlife department imported another 107 adults to be used as brood stock at the state game farm at Yerington. Between 1963 and 1979, biologists released 2,025 young in five locations.

Today, the Ruby Mountains are the only place in North America where snowcocks thrive. No one knows exactly how many there are, but the birds now occupy most of that range and have established breeding areas. There is also some scattered evidence that a few birds also remain in the East Humboldt Range, near the Rubies, and in the Toiyabe Mountains, in central Nevada.

The Nevada Department of Wildlife's census is limited mostly to incidental sightings while making helicopter surveys of big game, so an accurate count of the birds is not available. Gibson, who once worked for the department as a wildlife biologist, estimates that a total of 500 to 600 birds live in the area. That figures out to about one snowcock per square mile.

Hunting, which began on a limited basis in 1980, has virtually no impact on the population, according to Nevada wildlife biologist Sid Eaton. During the first four years, 91 known hunters only bagged 12 birds. To date about 80 birds have been registered with the department of wildlife. Gibson and his hunters have accounted for 32 of those birds.

Flying into Elko to meet with Gibson on an afternoon commuter flight from Salt Lake City, I had my first aerial look at the imposing Ruby Mountains. They jut straight up in corrugated relief from immense salt flats that look like used, dried chamois. The next morning the hunting party gathered at the trailhead on U.S. Forest Service land and loaded our gear onto pack horses and mules. It took most of the day for the animals to move us 10 miles, mostly up, to Gibson's tent camp at 9,800 feet.

At dawn we split into two parties for the 1,000-foot climb, a daily regimen, where horses couldn't go. Snowcocks, we were told, have eyesight as good as turkeys and they are just as wary. Therefore, it was recommended that we wear Desert Storm or ASAT camo patterned clothing, which blended perfectly with the brown-and-tan landscape. Our plan was to scale the peaks, using what cover we could find, slipping among shadows along the western slopes, until we reached a saddle and could peek over, looking for snowcocks. It was tough going.

During one of many rest stops, Gibson, who was leading Huneycutt, Kent and me on the ascent, whispered to us to chamber a shell (for safety, we had loaded only our shotgun magazines). Four snowcocks suddenly burst from a peak 500 yards away and sailed off toward our camp. Their song was a queer cacophony. Think of a meadowlark and a loon calling together, or, as Gibson says, a flute medley with rising and falling notes of *oodle, oodle, oodle.* I had heard nothing like this before.

"We'll never see those birds again," Gibson said. "They're spooked for good."

Two hours later and breathless, we made it to the top. Kent dropped into one basin and I to another while Gibson and Huneycutt elected to walk the saddles and peaks in an effort to drive birds past us. Like chukar, snowcocks typically run uphill and fly downhill, so it is possible to push them past shooters, a trick that British gunners learned a century ago in Asia.

Ever watchful from their lookouts, the birds' initial launch is a free fall--similar to a raptor's stoop--for 200 feet or more, until they flare their wings and begin alternately pumping and soaring. A typical flight is a half-mile to a mile, and it is nearly always from peak to peak.

All morning I waited in the shadows of a rocky ledge and glassed the surrounding precipices. Just before noon a Navy helicopter moved into the valley far below. The sound of its powerful blades reverberated on the canyon walls and spooked a dozen snowcocks off an outcropping. Through my 7X binoculars, I saw them roar past Kent a half-mile away and heard the booming miss of his gun. Then the birds glided past me, ghostly beige-and-white shapes calling in those odd bubbling sounds. They were twice out of range. Even if I had been in position and shot one, it would have fallen into a half-mile-deep canyon where I couldn't get to it.

Hours later the warm afternoon sun had me nodding off, but flute music suddenly awakened me. There the birds were--500 feet above and behind me on the very peak I had crossed that morning. Later, I found out they had landed on the other side of a huge stalagmite of rock and had walked to safety on the mountaintop. Their calling grew louder and more agitated, but I was fairly certain they hadn't seen me. Maybe Gibson and Huneycutt were coming up the other side of the mountain. Through binoculars I counted eight birds, three of which were roosters, or so their size suggested. I was as nervous as though glassing a full-curl ram.

The lead bird launched, pulling its wings into a Mach 2 tuck, and headed straight for me. The others pitched off close behind and suddenly the thin mountain air was full of musical calls and the flock came bearing down like fighter jets. They passed overhead at 50 yards--or was it 75? I picked the second bird, led by the length of a Buick, and fired. I'm sure now that I shot behind it, and the valley mockingly swallowed the gun's report. I watched the snowcocks soar on to Kent far below and saw one of the birds flare.

A full second later the roar of his gun reached back to me. He missed too.

That night around the campfire, Gibson said, "Well, two of you had an opportunity today. You saw birds, and you got some shooting. That's better than many hunters do."

It's true. One client hunted three years with Gibson, making 15 trips up and down those brutal mountain walls, and never killed a bird. The hunter gave up, admitted defeat and never came back.

After several days of climbing the Ruby's steep faces, I shared the frustration. I love hunting in land formed from tectonic and glacial wrenching. What I don't enjoy is the pain of getting there, and were it not for a bird or animal at the top, I wouldn't go.

But this is what makes the Himalayan snowcock so special. Perhaps the element of danger must be present for game to be considered a trophy. Although snowcocks don't attack like wounded Cape buffalo, jeopardy is never more than a step away.

For example, while scrambling over a talus, Lawson's feet suddenly went out from under him. Flipping over backwards, he rolled down the mountainside until his pack snagged on a rock and held him. His trousers were ripped open, and he smashed his hand on a rock. Bruised purple, his middle finger swelled to the size of a Ball Park frank.

On the fourth day, another helicopter, its cargo bay open and heat waves emanating from its engine, had driven a small knot of snowcocks from a canyon nook. Three birds piled into the basin where I had been hunting the first day. I watched them land on a rock spill near a big streak of shaded snow. White, our able-bodied guide, moved down to pick up Lawson while I climbed higher in an effort to pinch the birds. It didn't work. The birds saw us and, clucking in alarm, moved up and over the stony peak.

"Maybe they'll top out and wander into the next basin," White offered. "Let's go find out."

That meant negotiating the ominous "goat trail," a winding, wall-hugging ledge that narrows to only six inches wide in some places. With White leading, we crawled toward daylight on our bellies under ledges so narrow we had to remove our packs. Several times we handed unloaded guns and packs to each other. Along the way we encountered what White called the "death leap," an aptly named long step across a narrow slide of crumbled rock and soft earth. The worst spot, though, was an unnamed crack in the rocks where each man had to shimmy skyward, squeezing his way through the chasm and fighting for finger and toeholds. For a second I thought that I would fall, and a cup of adrenalin sluiced my brain.

"They're only birds," I thought to myself, gripping the rock wall, but the effort paid off. White was right--the birds had moved on to the next basin. He positioned Lawson and me where he thought that they would flush and then drove the birds over us. I shot at one but they were probably out of range, although it was hard to be certain.

On one of our last days in camp, Huneycutt, Gibson and I stalked a flock of feeding snowcocks to within 60 yards, but they flushed to safety while keeping a grove of pines between us. Later, Huneycutt and I kept vigil while Gibson circled the mountain between us. The ploy worked for Gibson, who shot a young rooster. That same afternoon Kent collected a mature bird by dropping one onto the saddle from a passing flock. Over two years he had shot a half-box of shells and made 12 trips up and down the peaks to bag his trophy. There were other opportunities during the five-day hunt, but those were the only birds our group managed to kill.

Although I was not among the lucky, I was not disappointed. I had been to the top of the world to hunt the ultimate gamebird. And now it is in my blood, and I know that I will have to go back.

5

A BOY'S FIRST TURKEY

By Ray Eye

Whenever anyone does something for the first time, it tends to go into a memory bank. You can replay an important first experience in your mind's eye time after time. I think God gave us this trait so that we could accept the inevitable passage of years with some happiness and appreciation. This is especially true with young boys and girls experiencing a brand-new adventure, whether it's a first date, a first trout, a first deer or, in this case, a first turkey. But there was something special about Ray Eye's first turkey. Even Ray didn't know how special it was until he was a young man. I won't spoil a good true story by revealing an ending that will give you pause.

y grandfather took one last sip of coffee, pushed his breakfast plate aside, and stood as he pulled out his pocket watch. "You'd better be going, boy, if you want to kill a turkey," he said, opening the lid of the old timepiece.

His words caught me so off guard that several seconds passed before I could stammer a reply. "But Pop [as he was always referred to in the Ozarks], aren't you going with me? I've never been turkey hunting before."

"I'd like to, Ray, but you know I've got chores to do," he answered, putting a hand on my shoulder. "Besides, the only way you're really going to learn is to get up there and do it by yourself. Now come on, you'd better get going."

I stood there in a state of shock and watched the old man leave the room to get his old Winchester 97 and a handful of shells. Following him to the back door, I still couldn't believe what was happening.

Just outside the door, he reached up and took down a kerosene lantern, scratched a match against its base, lit it, and handed it to me. "You know where to go on the mountain and what to do, boy. God knows, we've been through it enough," he said, stuffing the shotgun shells into my faded bib overalls. "Just remember what I've told you, and be careful." He placed the shotgun in my other hand and gave me a pat on the back that nudged me on my way.

Holding the lantern high, I headed across the yard, now more scared than excited. Those first few steps that I took as a 9-year-old were the toughest I've ever taken.

Some of my first memories are of the weekends spent on my grandparents' farm deep in the Missouri Ozarks. Located three miles up a valley, or "holler" as they call it in the hills, the farm had been the home of three generations of my family.

The white, two-story farmhouse was typical for the hills. A clear, spring-fed creek ran only a few yards from the front door, near the barn and other outbuildings. The house was set in a rare Ozark meadow, surrounded on three sides by steep evergreen and hardwood covered hills. The tallest of the hills was simply referred to as "the mountain," being one of the highest points in the state.

In 1962, the year I headed up the mountain that dark morning, most of America was in the middle of rapid modernization. Not so in the back country and around the farm. Life had changed little since my dad was born in the house decades before.

Electricity had just made it, but indoor plumbing hadn't, and the telephone never did. The roads were a far cry from what most folks were using. During the spring, the dirt path leading to Grandpa's turned into a muddy trough.

But there were advantages to living such a life. For one thing, it was simple. Everything consisted of hard work and doing the best you could with what was at hand. There was also a closeness shared between family and friends that sometimes slips away with progress.

The primitiveness of the mountains made them sanctuaries for wildlife. Small game was abundant, and deer and turkeys had never been pushed or shot out of the rough back country. Hunting was a part of life. Besides putting food on the table, it provided recreation. I loved it all, but turkeys held a particular fascination. They seemed to possess an almost mystical quality. They were rarely seen, but they were definitely there. I can remember one spring morning as though it were yesterday. Black storm clouds were marching over the mountain, and Pop and I were hurrying to get the last chores done.

With the first rumble of thunder came a gobble from a nearby ridge, and then another and another. I stood there, my mouth hanging open in amazement as the hills around the farm came alive with gobbles. Pop finally snapped me out of my trance, and we made it to the house just as the first of the big raindrops banged down on the tin roof.

Turkeys were constantly on my mind. In the woods, I was always looking for the birds and wanted to know what every piece of sign meant. I badgered poor Pop relentlessly, asking him to retell stories about turkey hunting when he was young. Looking back, he showed a great deal of patience and answered most of my questions to my satisfaction except for one: "When will I be old enough to hunt turkeys?"

"Someday," was his standard answer.

One fall day, his answer changed. The smell of homemade bread was in the air as we cut wood for the cookstove. Pausing to watch me work, Pop smiled and out of the blue said, "Ray, I think you'll be big enough by next spring." He didn't need to explain; I knew exactly what he meant.

A little later, he gave me what became my most prized possession--my own turkey call. Grandpa had made it by hand, using a piece of slate from the chalkboard at an old one-room schoolhouse. For a striker, he'd cut a piece of cedar from a fence post and fitted it in the bottom of a hollowed-out corncob.

The call was my life, and I practiced religiously. Teachers took the call away from me more than once for using it at school. Grandma said I sounded like "a cat caught in a fence," and Pop kept telling me to keep practicing.

The winter of 1961-62 was the longest of my life, but eventually it ended. Turkey season was only a week away when Pop shook me awake one cold April morning and said, "Get up, we're going up on the mountain for a while."

I did my best to keep up with him in the pre-dawn darkness as we crossed the creek, headed across the dew-covered pasture, and found the old trail that would take us up the mountain. We walked along quietly until we came to a huge oak at the junction of two ridges.

I started to ask one of the dozens of questions that were floating in my mind, but Grandpa quickly silenced me with a finger to his lips. He cupped his hands around his mouth and let loose an imitation of a barred owl. A turkey gobbled from down the ridge to the northwest.

We stood there for a while and listened to the sounds of turkeys gobbling from all over the hills. Each time one would call, the bird would rifle back a reply.

As we turned to leave, Pop whispered, "This is the place, boy. You'll want to sit with your back against that big oak, facing down that ridge. Use your call, and whatever you do, don't move until you're ready to come home."

The night before my hunt, I was a bundle of nerves and anticipation. Hoping to make the next day arrive faster, I slipped into bed after supper, dressed in my hunting clothes except for my oversized work jacket and old tennis shoes.

Sleep was hard to come by, and as I lay in bed I listened to the calls of the whippoorwills, the coyotes yipping on the mountain, and the steady sound of the stream flowing nearby. I'd been awake for hours when the smell of homemade biscuits and frying bacon and eggs drifted upstairs.

Normally, I'd have devoured the breakfast set in front of me in a matter of minutes, but not that morning. I picked at the meal and never took my eyes off Grandpa.

When he broke the news that I'd be hunting alone, I was heartbroken. For years I'd pictured us hunting together, and the thought of trying for one of the mountain's phantom birds alone was beyond my young imagination.

I tried to present myself as a man as I headed toward the creek. In some ways, it was the realization of a lifelong dream; I was going up on the mountain to try to kill a turkey. The fact that I was carrying Grandpa's favorite shotgun was an accomplishment. But inside, I was as scared as I'd ever been.

With my hands full, I had trouble crossing the stream, and midway across I missed a steppingstone and ended up standing knee-deep in the cold water. I made my way across the pasture, my wet shoes squeaking with every step.

I'd walked the trail to the top of the mountain dozens of times, but never had it seemed so long or so frightening. I finally arrived at the big oak, put out the lantern, and sat down.

I strained my mind to remember everything Grandpa had told me as I quietly slipped the blue paper shells into the pump gun. I sat there shivering from both cold and fear, desperately hoping that Pop would come walking up the trail.

With the reddening of the eastern horizon came the sounds of life in the timber. At first it was just songbirds, and I began to relax a little. Then came the eight-note call of a barred owl. I caught my breath when a turkey gobbled from down the ridge.

I picked up the slate call but couldn't use it. I was afraid--afraid I'd goof up and scare the turkey and ruin my dream. Again and again, I tried to rub the cedar against the slate, but each time I pulled back. Finally, I shut my eyes, swallowed the huge lump in my throat, and shakingly rubbed the peg against the little call. I winced at the gosh-awful noise it produced.

Whether it was in response to my call or just coincidence, I'll never know, but the gobbler sounded off. Several more times I tired to force some yelps from the call but I couldn't. I finally dropped the call in frustration and clutched the gun that was resting on my knees.

By then, I could hear turkeys gobbling all around me, the closest two being the bird in front of me and the tom on the next ridge. I waited and listened to their gobbling; I could tell they were not moving.

Suddenly, the soft yelps of a hen turkey came from behind me. I began to panic, fearing the hen would call the gobblers away from me. I started to get up to move closer to the hen, but suddenly I remembered Pop saying, "Whatever you do, don't move." Even though it looked hopeless, I stayed.

Soon the three birds were calling almost nonstop, and the two gobblers were heading my way. Then I began to realize that the hen was really a blessing. To get to her, the gobblers would have to walk right past me. Because I was too nervous to call, she was the only hope I had.

I could hear the two toms getting closer to each other, but I wasn't prepared for what came next. From just below the ridge came the loud noises of deep turkey purrs, flapping wings, and feathered bodies thumping together.

I didn't know it at the time, but the two birds were fighting for the hen. I was shaking so hard that I thought for sure the turkeys would see me, and the end of the gun barrel was drawing circles the size of doughnuts.

Hearing the sounds of limbs breaking, I watched as the big turkey rose through the trees and sailed out across the valley. A loud, triumphant gobble came from where the battle had occurred, and the hen rushed back a series of clucks and yelps. My pounding heart went into overdrive. My breathing was hard, and my black-rimmed glasses started to fog.

The next time the tom sounded off, he was so close that I could hear a rattle in his gobble. Like a ghost, he suddenly appeared to my right, head tucked back, feathers puffed out, and wings dragging on the ground.

My first response was to swing the gun and shoot, but in the back of my mind I heard Pop stressing, "Never move a muscle when you can see the turkey's head. If you do, he'll spot you for sure. Remember to aim just for the head."

Seconds seemed like hours, but I waited. When the bird stepped behind a big hickory, I twisted my body, cocked the hammer, and raised the gun. There was a deafening boom as the old gun went off when the turkey stepped back into view. In my haste, I'd tucked the stock under my arm, and the old Winchester had raised up and struck me in the face, bloodying my nose and sending my glasses flying.

Holding onto the gun with one hand, I rummaged through the leaves, found my broken glasses, and poked them onto my face as I ran to where I'd last seen the bird. My foot caught a root, and I tumbled down the ridge. When I finally stopped rolling, I looked up, and there he was, stretched out, his feathers glistening in the sun.

I arrived down at the farm, soaking wet, covered with mud and blood, half-dragging and half-carrying a turkey that weighed half as much as I did. Grandpa heard my shouts and was waiting for me.

He admired the bird, congratulated me, and then laughingly said, "You'd better run along and get yourself cleaned up before your grandma has a fit." I spent the rest of the day telling and retelling him how I'd killed the big gobbler, fibbing a little by telling him how I'd called the bird myself. He smiled and listened to every word.

A lot has changed since then. My life was never the same after I took that turkey. I was in the woods calling every spare minute I had. It cost me girlfriends, it cost me jobs, and it almost got me kicked out of school several times. But it was an addiction I wouldn't have stopped even if I could.

I learned a lot about calling turkeys that April morning, and I've learned a lot since. In fact, I've learned enough to make my living at it. I've guided for more than a decade and am now on the wild turkey pro staff of H.S. Strut, a division of Hunter's Specialties.

Grandpa and Grandma had to move off the farm and into a little community nearby. Grandma's still there and still kids me about sounding like "a cat caught in a fence." We lost Grandpa in 1976.

It wasn't long after his passing that the entire family was gathered at Grandma's. As usual, the talk turned to hunting, and someone brought up the subject of my first turkey. My eyes began to moisten, and I walked over and leaned against the fence to look out toward the mountain that held so many fond memories of Grandpa.

A few seconds later, I felt Grandma's hand softly rub my shoulder as she said, "You're thinking of Pop, aren't you?" Never taking my eyes off the mountain, I bit my lip and nodded my head.

She lovingly moved in beside me and softly said, "Ray do you remember that hen on the mountain the morning you killed your first turkey?"

I looked at her, swallowed hard, and said, "Yes."

"That wasn't a hen calling behind you," she said. "That was your grandpa."

6

PRINCE OF THE WOODLANDS

By Archibald Rutledge

Archibald Rutledge, the gentleman that he was back in the 1930s when he wrote such memorable tales of the game fields, called the ruffed grouse a superb game bird. He was right, of course, but I have a few other names for this bird. I think most ruffed grouse are sneaky, low-down critters that don't know the rules of bird hunting. If they knew the rules, these vengeful birds would wait until you got your other leg over the fence before flushing, they would flush up front and not wait until you turned your back, they would not fly off in a thunder of wings in front of your car as you cased your double. These "superb" game birds have done all these things to me and they have driven me to the point that I sometimes think I would shoot one in the back with no remorse. But then I remember the glorious years of grouse hunting in New England and I know down deep that I love that bird as much as Rutledge. I am sure you will enjoy these fine tales of grouse hunting as much as I.

While individual deer seem to develop rare intelligence, that sort of wisdom appears to be the possession of every member of the ruffed grouse tribe. I have known some deer to be simply dumb; some to be awkward and lumbering; some to be so curious as to be downright stupid. But in country where he has been long and persistently hunted, I have yet to see a ruffed grouse that is not always a shrewd tactician; and of course he is ever an aristocrat.

Oh, I have missed them--plenty of them, missed them coming and going, fore and aft. But since only the hits are history, I should like to record eight instances in which I have killed grouse--the whole constituting a kind of a case book ... Reading some of the very admirable articles on grouse by other sportsmen, I shall not be obliged to trespass on their preserves; for, while we have been after the same matchless game, my experiences have been radically different from theirs. For example, I have never had the privilege of shooting a grouse over the point of a dog. Our grouse in southern Pennsylvania are so scarce and so wary that they will hardly lie to a dog, however slow and cautious he may be. Our grouse seem on edge all the time; they are always wanting to go places suddenly in high gear. Our grouse shooting is practically all in the mountains, in heavy thickets, where tangles of grapevines riot over the lower trees; where old lumbering operations have permitted the second growth to make a wilderness of things; and where the footing is usually on slippery rocks ... All my grouse I have killed by walking them up; occasionally getting one on the first rise, but usually marking one down and following him with the greatest caution. Once in a long while I get a shot at one that another man has put up ... Well, here are the stories--true, even if I do happen to be the teller.

I. The Prince in the Golden Palace

Leaving my car in Johnson's Lane, which skirts the eastern edge of the Tuscaroras, I took a woods trail into the mountain about three o'clock on that golden autumn afternoon. The whole world hung like a ripe russet apple, and it smelled that way too. The air was still, damp, aromatic, fragrant with the scents of hickory-leaves, wild grapes, dewy mosses. The mystery of Indian Summer was over the world; and the woods were a golden palace, hung with gorgeous banners of flaming leaves. As I walked almost noiselessly up the old dandy trail that wound mazily into the mountain, I marveled at the beauty of it all; everything seemed saffron, and softly gleaming. Leaving the path, I followed upward the course of a little stream that had great green curtains of briars clothing the bushes and the lower trees on its banks. Of these berries grouse are very fond; and so dense is the cover that these vines afford that it is often possible to approach within twenty feet of a bird sheltered by one of these emerald canopies. But there were no birds in these briars that day. I turned aside into a golden dell, on the farther shoulder of which was a low growth or rock-oak and kalmia. While I paused for a moment to watch a gray squirrel, I heard a telltale chitter in the low laurels on the little hillock to the left ... Then I heard a grouse-note that was entirely new to me: it sounded like a soft yet distinct "Kruck-kruck-kroo-kroo." Then there came the inevitable little run in the strewn leaves, and my prince beat his way down the mountain.

In such a case I try with all the power of my sight and my hearing to get the bird's exact direction. When the woods are still, the hunter can often hear him alight. When not badly scared, and if the brush is fairly thick, a grouse may not fly a hundred yards; but he may go two. I have found that when he flies below the tree-tops, he likely will not go far. But if he once tops them, he may be bound for foreign lands.

I heard this one alight. Starting back toward him about twenty yards to the right of his course downhill, I found myself in an old road. By trying to keep a grouse on his left, the hunter will usually be afforded a better chance when the bird flushes. Two hundred yards I went, but nary a prince did I see. I turned and started back. I came on slowly and rather nonchalantly. Trying to creep often arouses this aristocrat's suspicion.

But my hope was almost gone when I came within fifty yards of the spot where the grouse had first risen. I stopped to look about. Somehow I had missed him. As I was peering to my right, from behind an old chestnut stump on my left he got up, starting straight away. There was a tattered screen of gold between us. I had just had a vision of that splendid tawny form hurtling like a projectile through the tinted woods. I saw that broad fan-tail with its beautiful banding of black. The only possible shot I had was one that depended for its effectiveness on co-ordination that was automatic. I must have covered the bird; for, while I did not really see him when I shot, I heard him fall. It was a lucky example of "dead" reckoning.

I found him lying on the gorgeous bed of leaves, a gorgeous thing himself--princely, unruffled of plumage. And I always recall that incident as a golden kind of thing--all golden--the woods, the plumage of my prize, and the nature of my good fortune.

II. A Wanderer

I suppose every grouse hunter remembers best the remarkable things that happened to him in following this superb game bird. One of the surprises of my life was the time I killed one when hunting quail. I was in some low brush along a creek, full four miles from the mountains. Quail were scattered in the cover. I had just crossed a wire fence and had turned toward the place where my dog was working when a grouse tore out of a patch of briars almost at my feet. I shot him almost before I realized what he was. How came he to be so far from his home in the hills? The creek flowed from the mountains; and undoubtedly, attracted by the abundant food and the good cover along its borders, he had wandered away from his habitat. That one bird in my bag meant more to me as I went home than the ten quail I had. In a sentimental way, I think a grouse outweighs a wild turkey.

III. The One I Tracked

It is easy enough to track a grouse in the snow; and to do so with killing intent is perhaps to take unfair advantage of him. But it is a different thing to track one across a sandy road. That October day it rained softly and insistently. About two o'clock the showers stopped. I drove out to the mountain and walked a little way down the sandy road that sags amiably through the brush at its foot. The road was still glistening from the rain, and from the bowed trees the water dripped heavily. Coming to a very clear stretch of sand, I saw where a grouse had apparently just crossed. He had been in the thickets next to the fields and was heading into the mountain. The little serrated fringes on his toes make a grouse's track readily identified. I studied carefully the exact line of his walk, and then looked into the forest on my left to see what cover might look attractive to my bird. Near the road great arras of greenbriars wept over a fallen cedar tree; a little farther on I saw lustrous bunches of wild-grapes hanging above a tangle of vines. A grouse will hardly pass up two such places.

But he was not in the briars. I recall feeling morally certain that he was under the grapes ... Grouse do not always fulfill one's ideas as to where they ought to be. But this one did. And he executed a maneuver against which the hunter always has to be wary. Instead of rocketing off in his customary slap-dash but unerring fashion, he elected to take to the air in a peculiar sliding and almost noiseless way. If I had not been certain that he was there, I never could have made the shot. As it was, I had to let drive through the tangle of vines, and I did not know the verdict until I picked him up on a carpet of vivid green moss some fifty yards from where I had shot. However, so great is this bird's momentum that his pitch often carries him many yards forward from that point in the air at which he is struck. I have known claims to be made of ninety-yard shots which were not, for the reason given, more than sixty-five or seventy.

IV. Old Transcontinental

Along certain stretches of our Conococheague Creek (which is respectable Indian for God knows what) there are few crossings. One reach of three miles offers one bridge only--and that a teetery, hold-my-hand affair. Yet beyond it is the best deer, turkey, and grouse country of all our mountains. Just beyond the bridge is a bare meadow; then fringes of alders and dense briars; then the open forest, sloping gradually upward. Game in these lowlands is very wild; not only because so many hunters cross that single bridge and go after it with early-morning zest; but because so many likewise, having bad luck higher up, and not caring much for those Mt. Everest expeditions, spend their time lazily combing these thickets. And it was here that, for a matter of three seasons, dwelt Old Transcontinental, a cock grouse that had furnished sport but no dinner to scores and scores of hunters. We christened him as we did because of his habit of flying farther than any other grouse that we had ever known. Pitching out of the gloomy recesses of a shrouded hemlock, that bird has flown full three-quarters of a mile--and I have seen him do it. Occasionally he would resort to the higher ridges, and launching himself from one of these, he would rocket down the mountain-slope at a speed and for a distance that were amazing. This was not only an excessively wary and far-traveling grouse; he was over-sized as well ...

Coming one day out of the turkey-woods with no gobbler slung manfully across my shoulder, walking rather wearily down an old road that ran through the lower thickets in which this matchless prince made his haunts, I was startled by having him hurtle suddenly from beneath a grapevine tangle and tear through the woods toward the meadow. It was only a hundred and fifty yards to that open stretch; and such a fly was far too short for this old champion.

Yet it did not seem likely that he would pass the cover of the thickets. If he stopped short, he would be in the low alders and tall briars on the meadow's edge. It looked like a chance for which I had waited in vain for three years. There was no mistaking his identity: he was too big, and this was his home.

I followed the road until I came out into the clear meadow. Then I turned to the left, keeping to the open. The bushes and briars that formed a margin to the woods were not over eight feet high, and they extended out into the meadow for a distance of about twenty feet. In this fringe my wily old voyager must be lurking. Out of the bushes at a rather critical place there rose a scarlet oak, the branches of which wept in characteristic fashion to the ground. Through that dense tangle of limbs I never could have made a shot; yet I had the feeling that Old Transcontinental would surely take the air just as soon as I got directly behind that obstruction between us. But round it I safely passed. If he got up now, I had a clear shot ... So few are the clear shots in our country at grouse that the chance for one is positively disconcerting. As in every other sport, in wing-shooting there is such a thing as being too tense ... Suddenly he roared out of the briars, executing a sort of spiral, the beveling of which gave him terrific momentum. Instead of going down over the briars, he headed straight into the dusky woods. At such a time there's always an aperture for which the bird is heading; and if the hunter is lucky in guessing *which* aperture, the game is his. I managed to cover a likely hole just as the cock did, and he plunged headlong. This was a magnificent specimen in full plumage; yet my triumph was tempered by the thought that I had robbed those woods of a real personality.

V. The Orquic Valley Ghost

There's game of ghostly beauty--albinos; and they appear in practically all forms of wild life. But I had never seen a snow-white grouse until a forest ranger told me of one that had haunted the hemlock-hung hollows of Orquic Valley, which lies just outside the Buchanan Game Reserve. For at least two seasons this extraordinary bird had been reported; and after I learned of his existence I was told by hunters that they had been after him in real earnest. But like most other birds or animals of this spectacular coloring, this grouse was so shy that he was rarely seen and more rarely shot at. One man told me that he had seen the bird in a pine tree, but had taken it for an owl. When he was fifty yards past it, this prince in ermine rocketed down the long lonely valley away from him, its glimmering form at last fading from sight against the distant tree-tops ... Such a bird seemed to me worth a special trip into the wilds of Orquic, which is typical Pennsylvania deer-country; a primeval vale between two immense ridges, strewn to the very top with boulders. Yet despite the rocks the place is heavily timbered. Down the laureled gorge dashes a trout-stream ... For many miles there is no human habitation.

This adventure represents a thing in hunting that all experienced sportsmen have found to be true: however wild your game may be, if you stay with it, your great chance will surely come. The only question is, How long can you stick?

My trek after this grouse of the snowy plumage was an all-day affair, and I must spare details. About two miles down Orquic Valley, some three hours after I had begun to hunt, I jumped him out of a wild melee of old logs and grape-vines ... Now while he was the very thing I was hunting for with all my heart and soul, let me confess that when he jumped, I did not even shoot at him. You know how it is: sometimes the mind plays queer tricks. Occasionally mine tells me, at the critical moment when my gun should be in action, that, at last, the game is *found* ... Meanwhile he is getting away on burning wings. I just stood there and watched with amazement and something akin to awe the bewildering beauty, grace, and speed of that patrician of patricians ... I almost forgot to mark where he was going!

I flushed him on one slope of the broad valley; his flight took him clear across to the other ridge. I thought I saw him go down by a clump of burly rock-pines ... In that neighborhood, gentlemen, all over those treacherous rocks, under and over logs and smothers of vines, up and down dale, even across the immense ridge I faithfully rambled. But the prince with the ermine coat I utterly lost. He was either a smart bird or I was a dumb hunter--probably both. During my milling around I flushed a half-dozen other grouse. These I passed up, and then, as my Great Hope began to wane, I cursed this practice of passing things up.

The sun had begun to stretch out the hills when I turned homeward. As a hunter often will, I decided to go back by the place where I had first roused my game ... I might find a white feather to take home. He had certainly burst through those vines with vigor enough to strip himself of all plumage ... At last I came to the wild vineyard. Certain sere leaves on the rock-oaks were whispering, and that natural sound must have deadened my footfalls. I came to the very tangle out of which my snowy bomb had exploded ... I foolishly and vainly peered in the place for sight of a feather. This I was doing when the albino bird itself burst from the dense vines out of which I had startled him seven hours before. He went off at a crazy tangent, and I led him about two feet. To my surprise he fell at the shot; and when I retrieved him, he entirely fulfilled all my ideas of a dream-prince. This bird is always aristocratic and immaculate. What shall be said of one whose plumage is like new-fallen snow? Of all the wildwood trophies I have ever secured, this one was the handsomest, and secured under the most peculiar conditions.

How had he come back to his starting point? In this part of the country grouse are in the habit of flying to their favorite feeding-ground; and while I had been searching for him half a mile away, unseen by me he had flown back across the valley to his beloved grape-vines.

VI. The Prince in the Pines

In the wilds of Path Valley, where the mountains lie on either hand in mighty folds there's an immense old field, in the center of which is a pine thicket some five acres in extent. These trees are not more than twenty feet high; many of them are half blown over. Going through them is like trying hard to get lost. Such a place is often resorted to both by deer and grouse. I saw grape-vines in this shadowy fastness, and these looked promising. Soon I was lost in the dusky silence of this strange grove. A dim trail led through this fragrant sanctuary, and down this I warily walked.

Some six or seven yards from the farther end I heard a grouse get up and go roaring off toward the ravine below the pines. I dashed to the edge of the thicket, got my gun up, and fired at the far-fleeing bird just as he was clearing the tops of the hardwood trees on the brink of the gully. Down he came--a fortunate shot, and pure luck, of course. I later discovered when he was dressed that just one shot had struck him, but that was in the back of the head.

VII. A Wily Patrician

One day I was hunting at Webster's Mills with two of my sons--
that place being within a few miles of Hancock, Maryland. The
Mills perhaps have been or may be, but at present they aren't. My
boys had gone ahead of me, greatly excited over the fresh spoor of
a bear. I was sitting on a pine stump, the mellow sunlight filtering
over me and through me. Suddenly I hear a grouse get up. The boys
had flushed him, and he came straight back for me. I saw him
hurtling headlong toward me, and was just about to get out of his
way when he banked and came to earth just about twelve feet from
me. I have noticed that when a grouse alights after having been
alarmed, he nearly always runs for the nearest shelter. In this case
he dodged in beside an old log. He was out of sight, but there he
was. And there I was. I figured that he had not made me out. What
to do in such a case is a little puzzling. The place was thick, and the
chance for a deft get-away exceedingly good. But to my right were
hemlocks and birches and a stream. It was toward them that the
bird had been headed. When flushed again, he would doubtless
take up his old route. For five minutes I studied the situation,
trying to put myself in the place of the bird. At last I made up my
mind just where he was going ... Oh, Man! Never make up your
mind that you know what an intelligent wild critter is gwine do.
What keeps him alive is his ability to keep you guessing. I rose from
the stump and was ready for a right-hand shot toward the hemlocks.
But no. That grouse slid off the ground with hardly any more noise
than an owl that had just had his hinges greased would make. He
just snaked himself off, very low to the ground, deftly threading the
glimmering thicket. I let drive hopelessly, but he fell. It really
wasn't fair. He had fairly outwitted me, but had lost the game ... I
remember that grouse because he always makes me think that to
kill this bird the hunter should make an especial study of its styles
of flight. There's an infinite variety--from the stormy explosive rise
to this eerie moth-like performance; but always there is a kind of
dizzy precision and a high-gear speed, even in the thickest timber,
that puts this bird in a class by itself, and will thrill the heart of any
hunter, however seasoned.

VIII. The Prince in the Mist

I was turkey-hunting behind Hogback Mountain. It was just
daylight, but a radiant mist was over the world, and in the deeper

hollows it was still banked in mysterious folds. I had both barrels loaded with chilled 2's. Coming to an ancient charcoal heart, which in the Pennsylvania woods are favorite places for both hunters and game to reconnoiter, I stood there looking out over the wild valley, with the immense rocky flank of Hogback to my right. No one knows why those things happen so, but this one did, and is now a part of my hunting history. Across the gleaming vale I saw a shape coming at lightning speed; another, even swifter, was following. It was a big cock grouse, with a goshawk after it. They were at least seventy yards up, but were coming almost over me. I just had time to get my gun up. Leading the grouse almost a yard, I touched the trigger; then gave precisely the same attention to the tawny pursuer. By some miracle both birds plunged downward; and when I found them they were not ten yards apart. I supposed I should have let the lordly grouse go; but in hunting, as in most things mortal, instinct is stronger and more immediate than sentiment.

Such is the true history of eight of the princes of the woodland that I have secured. If I were to record the tale of those I had missed, my story would be much longer.

7

NAT'S DOG

By Joan Tyler Fairbanks

It's hard to say what special quality makes an outdoor story a classic. Whatever it is, this story has it. Joan Tyler Fairbanks is a new author to me, but I know I'll never forget her name or story. "Nat's Dog." Joan's first story, appeared in Sports Afield in 1985, and after reading it, I knew it belonged in this book. It's a story about a special woman and an exceptional dog, and how they both handle a certain problem. If you can read this without shedding a few tears or getting a big lump in your throat, I can only assume that you missed out on the best part of life. I mean love, of course.

ll winter, spring, and summer Nat's dog had waited for him to come home. For hours each day she had sat in front of the picture window in the living room hoping for the sound of his truck tires on the gravel drive, the banging of the old Chevy door, May's voice calling brightly, "Nat, that you?"

She had seen the seasons change from her spot by the window. The first snowflakes falling gently, then faster and faster until they covered the ground with a paper-thin white icing. The big nor'easter that began the day after Christmas and continued fierce and howling for 48 hours, leaving the house all but buried and May stranded for two more days until the plows got through.

Then winter had gentled into spring and the rains came and the world beyond the window was brown and muddy. When May would let her out in the morning she would pad carefully around the puddles, but still her snow-white paws were chocolate colored and slick, and May would carefully wipe them with an old towel so as to keep the carpets clean. This too passed, and one morning the rain stopped, the sun broke through, the sky was azure, and the air was sweet with summer again. And Nat's dog waited by the window, and still Nat did not come home.

Where he had gone and why he did not return remained a mystery to her, for she was, after all, only a dog, and dogs do not understand the meaning of tears, and of neighbors bringing casseroles and pies, and of Nat's old friends coming and holding May close and whispering, "I'm so sorry." A dog could not know that when Pete, the oldest son, had burst in the door that cold November day, his face ashen, his voice broken, and cried, "Mom, it's Pop!" that Nat Walker would never come home again.

She had greeted each one of his old friends hopefully. Perhaps he was with Joe, or Steve, or Mike, as he had been so many times before when he had left, only to return, sometimes days later, his rifle tucked under his arm, his red plaid hunting jacket smelling of the woods and fields. Then all would be right again in her world. May would make coffee and put out a plate of doughnuts, and the dog would sit under the table while Nat's friends slipped her pieces of the sweet cakes until Nat would say, laughing, "Whoa, now. That's enough, old girl. You'll be fatter than those partridge you keep telling me are out there." Then she would come out from beneath the table and lie by Nat's side and smell the familiar woodsy smells emanating from his clothes until it grew late and all the stories of the hunt were told and told again.

One day her heart leapt when she heard Nat's truck coming up the drive, and she raced to the door, barking joyfully. At last he had come. Where he had been for so long did not matter. He was here now, and she forgave him. But it was not Nat, only Mike, his oldest friend and hunting companion who had come to talk with May.

"Glad I bought the old truck," Mike said as he approached the doorway. "It's good for bumping down dirt roads. How are you doing, May?"

"Okay," she answered. "I get through each day somehow. The nights are the hardest."

"It doesn't mean much, I know," Mike said gently, "but he died doing the thing he liked best. I guess pulling that deer was just too much for him. The old fool just wouldn't wait until we got there to help."

"It was the way he would have wanted it," May agreed. "But it doesn't make it any easier for the boys and me."

"I don't like to think of you all alone out here," Mike said, "the boys living so far away and all. If you need anything, just give Marion or me a call, will you?"

May had nodded her head slowly.

"Thanks, Mike. Actually I was thinking of going south next winter. Staying with my sister. But I don't know about the dog."

"Maybe you could give her away," Mike suggested. "I'd take her myself, but she would never hunt for anyone but him. I've got three as it is anyway. Not to mention the fact that Marion would shoot me."

May had smiled, remembering. Even when she herself had gone out with them, the dog never would give the bird over to anyone but Nat.

"No," May had said slowly. "I wouldn't expect you to take her. Likely as not I'll just keep her. She's getting older. She probably couldn't adjust."

When spring came Nat's dog had been sure he would come home. Spring meant fishing, and Nat loved to fish. They would leave very early in the old truck, slipping quietly out of the house into the misty dawn while May slept. Nat would drive to his secret spot and stop the Chevy. "You stay," he would say to his dog. "I'll be back soon." And she would wait patiently until she saw him coming out of the brush, his old fishing basket dangling at his side and full of trout. But spring passed, and he did not come to fish.

She expected him in summer. Summer had always meant long, lazy afternoons and gold twilight evenings bass fishing at the lake. On Friday nights in the summer he would come in from work and call out, "Who wants to go to camp?" and she always knew the words and would race madly around the house, her stubby tail wagging until it ached. May would have everything ready and Nat would load it in the back of the pickup and off they would go, the three of them, to Nat's camp. But summer passed, and still he did not come. But she never doubted.

It was in the autumn that she knew he would, though, for autumn was their time. The best time. The time when he would take down his Winchester 12-gauge and carefully clean it, and she would sit by his side watching him, shivering with excitement.

"Tomorrow's the day," he would say. "Going to get birds, are you?"

She knew the phrase "going to get birds." She would whine and dance around on her snow-white feet, and he would laugh and ruffle her head gently. The next day, when the October dew had lifted from the grass and the weakening sun had warmed the brambles and thickets, he would call to her, "Time to get birds!" and off they would go into the woods behind the house, just the two of them usually. They would hunt until the shadows grew long and the sun sank behind the hills in the field.

So now it was October, and she was sure he would come home. She waited by the window hour after hour, day after day, watching, listening, never giving up hope.

May sat in the living room chair day after day and watched the dog grow thinner and thinner. The dog seldom ate anymore, and then only enough to keep herself alive. May had tried tempting her with bits of beef and chicken, but she only licked them once or twice and then left them in her dish.

"I know how she feels," May thought at as she forced herself to eat and sleep and go about her life, trying to put it back together. She didn't cry. She had not cried. Not once, even when she knew that thirty-eight years of being Nat Walker's wife had ended abruptly on a cold, gray November afternoon. Sometimes she was mad at him for leaving her, but she could not cry. She wondered if people thought that was strange. Probably they figured she cried herself to sleep at night. Most likely they said to each other, "Poor May. Look how brave she is."

So now it was October, almost a year. October was the time she equated most with Nat Walker because it was on a crisp, fresh October evening forty years before, when she was eighteen, that she had met him at the Windsor Fair Dance. He was handsome, and full of laughter and fun, but he was a Walker, and the Walkers were known for being independent and even a little wild at times. She had resisted and tried not to fall in love with him, but the following October she became his wife.

On their first anniversary he had presented her with a Remington 26-gauge. It was not quite what she had expected, but she knew why he had done it and acted pleased anyway. Sometimes, in the first years, she even went out with him on those sharp, clean fall days when the birds were fat and plentiful in the woods behind their house. Then Pete was born and then Mark and then Tim. She stayed home with the children and was secretly just as glad. Still, every year he would carefully clean her gun and hang it beneath his on the rack. "In case you decide to go out," he'd say, and once in a while she would. He was proud that she was a fair shot and boasted of it to his friends. He did not tell them she was a good mother, or that she made great blueberry pies, or that she could sew him a flannel shirt that was equal to anything L.L. Bean sold. No, he told them she was a fair shot. And she understood and knew he loved her.

It was one of those sunny Indian summer afternoons when the air is heavy with the musky smell of fallen leaves and there is an urgency in the calling of birds flying overhead that May Walker sat in her living room and stared first at the thin, mournful dog sitting by the window and then at the old Remington hanging on the rack. She remembered how he had given it to her, and she remembered when he had come in that cold winter day, almost nine years before, with a small bundle wrapped in his sweater and tucked under his arm.

"What's that?" she had asked.

"Present for you," he had said, and handed her the sweater. It had wiggled, and a small head had popped out from a sleeve.

"Oh, Nat," she had said. "I thought we agreed! No more dogs after Snook went."

"It's one of Bill Lee's bitch pups," he had told her. "Bill gave her to me. How could I refuse? I didn't want to hurt his feelings. Besides, this is a Brittany. She won't get as big as Snook."

The puppy licked her hand. Nat grinned and the dog stayed.

May got up from the chair and took her gun down from the rack. She ran her hands over the fine walnut stock and thought how Nat's hands had been the last to touch it.

The dog pricked up her ears and watched. For a moment her heart soared. Guns meant birds, and birds meant Nat. But it was not Nat holding the gun. She laid her head on her paws and sighed. May stared at the dog and at the gun and then out the window, where a breeze was swirling the orange and red maple leaves.

"Come on," she said. "Let's get birds."

The dog leapt to her feet. She knew those words. She forgot her misery--the instinct was just too powerful and the years of training too well done. She danced around happily as May donned her jacket and tucked some shells into the pocket. May loaded the gun and opened the door. Together they went out to hunt partridge.

The first leaves were crackly beneath their feet, but as they entered the woods there was a sweet dampness in the air, and they walked almost silently on the leaf-padded ground. The dog ranged ahead at just the distance Nat had taught her. Her nose caught each passing breeze as she moved carefully back and forth across the path. Suddenly she found what she was looking for. She tested the air one more time and snapped to a point.

May came up quietly and motioned her into the brush. She leapt forward, and there was a whir of wings as a bird whistled into the sky. May lifted the gun and shot, and the bird fell heavily. The dog waited until May motioned her after it. She bounded joyfully into the brush at the signal.

It did not take long for her to find the bird. Gently she picked it up, and began carrying it back. Her eyes were bright, and her heart was beating with anticipation. Now Nat would come. He would be there to take the bird. His hands would stroke her head and his voice would say, "Good old girl." She broke from the brush and looked for him.

May stood with her hand outstretched.

"Give," she said. The dog looked around, confused. Where was he? He had always been there to take the bird. She sat down to wait.

"Give," May said again.

The dog sat unmoving and stared at May stubbornly.

"Damn you, give," May cried. "Don't you understand? He's gone. He's not coming back. It's just us now. Do you hear me? Give!"

The dog looked at the woman whose hands had fed her all her life and brushed her and treated her when she had cut herself on barbed wire or low brambles. She looked for Nat again. He was not there. "Give" echoed in her mind, and the years of training told. Slowly she got up and approached May. Gently she laid the partridge in May's outstretched hand. She looked into the woman's face and waited.

"Good girl," May sobbed. "Oh, good old girl!" And she threw her arms around Nat's dog. The dog rested her head on May's shoulder and gently licked her ear.

"Oh, Natty, Natty," May sobbed over and over again.

After a while the crying stopped, and she wiped her eyes with her jacket sleeve. She drew a deep breath and pushed her hair from her face. She got up slowly and picked up the Remington Nat had given her 38 Octobers before.

"We'll both love him till the day we die, old girl," she said. "But we'll get by. We'll go on."

The dog slowly wagged her stubby tail. Somehow she understood. He was not coming back. His gentle hands would never touch her again. She would never hear his voice or see his face. But they would go on. She understood as best a dog can.

May reached down and stroked the dog absentmindedly. The tears had finally come. The terrible ache was gone. There was a loneliness in its place that she knew she would feel forever, but the pain was gone.

"Come," she said. Together, she and Nat's dog went on into the cool October woods to get birds.

8

THE OLD MAN AND THE TOM

By Charles Elliott

Long before there were "turkey-hunting experts," there was Charlie Elliott. Charlie is the acknowledged "grandfather of modern turkey hunting." Few writers have influenced their readers more strongly. When he once mentioned that slamming his car door had provoked a tom to gobble, hunters around the country followed suit in an effort to locate their spring birds.

As an editor for Outdoor Life, Charlie has provided a wealth of much more conservative turkey-hunting wisdom, as well. Turkeys, turkey hunters, and the times have surely changed, but at more than 80 years of age Charlie Elliott can still do what he always did best; hunt gobblers and write about them. After all these decades, this story may have been the most difficult for him to write. One of his letters to me reveals why, and I want to share it with you because it also reveals the spirit of one of the best outdoor writers in the business:

"Dear Vin,

I finally dug my spurs in and wrote this turkey piece we talked about. I'm just now getting back on my feet after that siege I had with the medics more than a year ago....For a while I was afraid I'd live-- I feel good enough now to be afraid I won't. I figure I should be well on the way to reasonably good shape for an old hunter. On the other hand, I guess I'll end up like I told Polly the other day--probably the last thing I'll ever do is crawl across my office floor, reach up, and hit the wrong key on the typewriter.--Charlie" f he lives alone, or lives long enough, an outdoorsman is likely to arrive at a certain stage of life when he begins to talk to himself. Whether he's lonely, or beyond his allotted span, or has slipped a cog in the upper story, thinking out loud seems to help solve whatever problem he has at hand.

At the moment, though, there was no mite of satisfaction in the castigation I was heaping upon myself.

"You're an old fool. Your eyes wouldn't let you see an ostrich if one stepped on your toes. You couldn't hear a jet plane if it flew close enough to knock off your face mask. You have hardly enough lung capacity to blow your nose, and your legs get wobbly if you walk to the mailbox. By what stretch of the imagination do you think you can hear, call up, see, and bag a wild turkey gobbler?"

It really wasn't that bad, but it was the way I felt at the moment. Yet there I was, perched on a mountain slope in turkey woods, trying to recapture some of the golden moments of other years when my senses were strung like a tight bow string.

For more than sixty years, few seasons had come and gone that I didn't bring home one or more gobblers. Two years ago, that special utopia suddenly became a thing of the past when old age caught up with me and I fell on hard physical times. For months, my medical insurer and I kept a couple of hospitals in business and provided several medical men with good vacations. Somehow, my eighty-plus-year-old-hide and the carcass inside it survived the cutting and chemicals, but I had lost more than my share of turkey-hunting days.

At the opening of this new gobbler season, I was a long call from being loaded with vim and vigor, as I had been in other days not too far behind me. I had not lost my awareness of how necessary it is for a man to have his senses sharp and working if he expects to compete with an old feathered Einstein.

With me were two companions whom I considered among the most knowledgeable turkey hunters in the country. I had hunted with each over many seasons. Roscoe Reams has been a regular companion for more than forty years, and we've shared many splendid hours in the woods. My other partner, Frank Piper, is on my list of most favorite Yankees. He owns and operates Penn's Woods Products, a national manufacturer of calls and other turkey-hunting equipment.

Each of these hunting mates had been thoughtful enough to pull me aside and privately propose that because my physical equipment was not up to par, he go along as my eyes and ears and call my bird close enough for me to see and shoot.

To each proposal, I explained: "I really appreciate this, but it won't be the same unless I do it on my own. Maybe I can find a bearded one as retarded and decrepit as I am."

They had respected my wish, gone up another trail, and left this neck of the mountain to me.

We were smack in the middle of one of those mysterious periods that tom turkeys go through without gobbling. The mating season may be in full swing, the temperature perfect, the barometer high, the birds known to strut and the hens to go to them, but sometimes when every condition seems perfect, the gobblers clam up for a few days for no apparent reason.

The first two mornings of the season, I left the high country to my partners and devoted my efforts to the lower ridges around the little valley. I called and listened from a half-dozen points that I could climb without splitting my spleen but heard no gobbling. Higher on the mountain, both Frank and Roscoe saw turkeys feeding but could get no vocal response from the birds.

"Since there's no way I can keep up with you jackalopes on these mountain slopes," I told them on the second day, "I follow the next best procedure I know--calling, waiting, and hoping.

The first gobbler I ever bagged was from this region in 1923, and over the years of hunting since then, I was well acquainted with the territory. Around Roscoe's camp, I knew those coves in which the birds fed regularly. Also pinpointed were several roost sites where we never failed to find birds early in the season.

Because my climbing was limited, my best bet was to set up shop along one of the most popular travel routes between the dinner table and the bedroom limbs and call just enough to interest some gobbler with a craw full of curiosity.

I could only guess how the turkeys felt about it, but I thought that the spot I had selected was ideal. I arranged my blind in the edge of the open hardwoods along a small creek. If the torn earth was any indication, several large coves on both sides of the creek below must have been abundant with acorns, grubs, and other choice tidbits of a turkey's diet. The feeding area channeled into a narrow passageway along the creek to the roost site on the ridge.

For most of my turkey-hunting life, I constructed my blinds out of dead tree limbs, brush, live foliage, or whatever material I happened to find on the spot that could be arranged to break my outline. In the past three or four years, I have found it much less time-consuming to carry a camouflage net blind, arranged on lightweight stakes that can be easily shoved into the soft earth to hide my body so that only my head shows. This gives me the opportunity to shift my legs or buttocks when they grow numb or painful from long waiting in an exposed position. The cloth blind hides the lower part of my anatomy more effectively because I tend to be the wiggle-worm type.

If you use your eyes, ears, and a little bug juice in the proper places, a most delightful period that anyone can spend is sitting quietly in the woods, watching the endless play of drama and comedy of the wild citizens around you. The anticipation of hearing or seeing an old longbeard at any moment adds suspense to the sights and sounds of small birds moving through the trees with the muted music of a creek in the background.

All of this was pleasant, the afternoon was warm, and I struggled to overcome the usual routine of an after-lunch nap in my favorite easy chair at home.

"Patience," I kept repeating. "Have patience. It's a turkey hunter's most useful asset."

Old age, or the nap habit, prevailed. For how long I don't know, but I opened my eyes suddenly. Either instinct or a lifetime of training kept me from moving my head. Seven hens and a small gobbler scratched the open woods in front of me. The jake seemed to be the only one of the flock curious about my blind. He moved cautiously toward it, a step or two at a time, and once he might have been within range, but with my poor depth perception I wasn't sure, so I didn't try him.

When the flock scratched on across the open woods and out of sight, I clucked softly, waited a few minutes, then yelped. There was no answer, but soon the hens and jake came back. When it appeared that they would again feed by, out of range, I tried another tactic. I gave what I considered a reasonable imitation of the *burr-rr-rr-r* call, used when the birds seem to greet or talk with one another. This got the flock's attention. Heads went up, and then it seemed that the entire group was talking. The birds didn't come any closer to my blind, but went slowly on up the creek, *burr-rr-rr-ring* and clucking to one another in a conversational tone, known to the mountaineers as *cacking*. When a flock carries on in this manner, it is an indication that the birds are undisturbed and at ease.

It was a nice show, a sort of rerun from other days, and I enjoyed it with no sense of disappointment that I had not tried the young gobbler at a questionable range.

I settled down with my back to the tree, watched and listened for a while, and dozed again. One of the special quirks of an otherwise normal turkey hunter is that all of the rest of his body can go sound asleep in a turkey blind, but his ears never do. They filter out the usual forest sounds and file them away as unimportant, but any noise that could possibly be made by a turkey rings an alarm in his brain.

How long I slept, I do not know. A cluck woke me. A large gobbler came into focus, and I sat motionless while he walked slowly out of range. I was somewhat surprised that he was moving downstream, away from the roost site on the mountain. But he seemed in no way disturbed.

When he was out of sight, I clucked a couple of times. A few minutes later, I yelped softly. I followed this after a short interval with a series of lusty yelps. For more minutes, I strained for an answer that never came. More in frustration than in hope, I gobbled the box like an old tom turkey mad at the world. The only result was the derisive caw of a crow down by the creek.

My inclination of the moment was to give it up and walk to camp, but once more I told myself: "Patience! Have patience, like you advise everyone else. You're in a good location. You've seen turkeys. Stay put!"

I didn't call any more. There are two schools of thought on calling. One says that you should continue to cluck and yelp to attract any bird passing by. The other school, to which I belong, thinks that once a turkey has you pinpointed, he will eventually arrive to investigate.

That must be the only reason that kept the seat of my pants compatible with the roots, rocks, and contour of the ground under the tree against which I sat.

I take no credit for character. In spite of all this, I was on the very verge of standing up, gathering my gear, and taking the trail to that bourbon and branch water when the gobbler that had strolled by less than an hour earlier was suddenly in front of me. Without making a sound, he had sneaked back, apparently looking for the source of my calls.

He walked very slowly, but with every movement showed how alert he was. When his eye disappeared behind a tree trunk, I put the gun to my shoulder, and when he appeared again, my sights were on his neck. I held them there until he paused suddenly, almost in the middle of a stride, his head high and suspicious. Praying that my judgment of distance was correct and that he was within range, I squeezed off a shot.

The gobbler half-fell on his side, then regained his balance and roared upward on wings that carried him at an angle across the slope. He was in the trees before I could get off another shot. I stumbled over the edge of the blind and ran a few steps to get a line on the course of his flight, but he was out of sight. I stood still and listened for him to crash or to hear his dying flutter, but heard nothing.

I knew that the bird had been hit hard because I found neck feathers where he had stood when I shot. For more than an hour, I combed that mountain slope in the direction the bird had flown. I climbed to look at limbs or piles of debris that might have been my turkey. I looked under logs, around laurel thickets, but not a feather could I find. Heartsick to the core at wounding such a magnificent bird, I took the trail to camp.

I was glad to find that Roscoe had come in early. I gave him a blow-by-blow of my unhappy experience.

"We've got about thirty minutes of daylight left," I suggested. "Why don't you carry your eyes back up there with me for a last look?"

"I was hoping you'd ask," Roscoe said.

We were on the trail about a hundred and fifty yards from where I had shot the turkey when Roscoe commented casually, "I know what happened to your bird."

"Wh-what?" I stammered. "What?"

He made no reply but walked on ahead of me for forty yards and picked up my gobbler. It was lying beside the trail, partly hidden in the leaves. With my defective eyesight, I'm sure I never would have seen it.

Weighed on the scale in Roscoe's cabin, the gobbler was a twenty-pounder. It sported a slightly-over-nine-inch beard.

"Well," I said, "that does it. I'm just too damned old and infirm to hunt gobblers anymore."

Roscoe grinned. "We've got one more day here," he said. "You've taken only half your season limit. What time do you think we should get up in the morning?"

9

LINGERING GREATNESS

By Floyd A. Baker

Everyone loves a dog story, especially a story about an old hunting dog. I'm not going to say much more about "Lingering Greatness," except to say that after you read it, you'll probably want to give your dog a hug--even if he busts birds in the fields, hunts by himself, can't find cripples, and generally embarrasses you in front of your hunting buddies. He's still "your hunting dog."

The last half of December had been much colder than usual, and early January wasn't much better. After finally forcing myself to go outside and do the usual farm chores one cold morning, I decided that it would be at least 1 or 2 P.M. before a person would have any business trying to find a few quail.

I owned a pointer bitch that was about five years old and that I believed to be among the better dogs. I had also just started a Brittany pup of about six months that had enough natural ability to make most men brag a little about their dog training, even if unjustified. Dog men and fishermen seem to possess bragging ability now and then.

I had seen many quail seasons come and go, and several good dogs, long gone, linger in my memory--dogs that never loafed on the job. They were always willing partners, no matter how hard the conditions.

I wonder, sometimes, if the dogs we remember as less than great just never understood what we really wanted because our training could have been better. It is always easier to lay the fault on the dog, I guess.

On dark, cold, and dreary days, thoughts such as these seem to find their way into our minds--or maybe they come to mind because we're getting a little older and we reminisce more.

I looked out the window one more time around noon and saw that the sun had finally come out. It looked warmer, anyway. I had a quick bite to eat and stepped out to check the weather again. The wind was still blowing from the north, ten or fifteen miles an hour-- not the best day for hunting I had ever seen. But after being unable to hunt for several days, I decided to try it for a little while.

I tried to think of someplace where there was still a covey or two that wouldn't be harmed if I took three or four birds. I remembered an old field that bordered on quite a bit of timber. A pretty good creek ran through the north end of the area. There had been a couple of coveys there earlier in the season, but they had given me the slip after I had taken only four or five birds with twice as many shots.

There was plenty of cover in the field and maybe the birds would hold. That's what that pup needs, I thought, after the wild birds we had hunted last. I would take him by himself. It would do him good. He hadn't hunted alone before.

I put more clothes on than I thought a man could shoot in, and after I loaded the pup in the truck, I decided that an extra pocketful of shells wasn't a bad idea. No one would be there to see how many shells I used.

I drove the four or five miles in about ten minutes. When I parked the truck by an old gate, a feeling of excitement began to make me forget about the cold. I opened the door of the dog box and that bundle of energy leaped out. The pup seemed a little confused and ran in circles, coming back to see where the old dog I had left at home was. The pup was, I guess, uncertain as to whether he could handle the job alone. But after we had walked more than half of the 30-acre field, he was hunting very well. We searched every acre pretty thoroughly, but failed to find one single bird. The cold spell had caused them to change their range, I thought. The pup had hunted everywhere in the old field.

Heading toward the truck, I noticed clouds covering the sun--the kind of clouds that seem to make the cold seep in through your boots and around the collar of your jacket. I looked south, across the country road where I had parked, toward some rolling hills. There was probably a half mile of bare pasture land between me and the hillside farther to the south. I hated to go home without giving the little dog a chance to see what he could do by himself.

Crossing the road, I headed him south. The walk would do us both good, I thought to myself. Besides, two or three weeks earlier, a hunting friend and I had set a good covey near a pond at the base of those ridges and there should be several birds still in that bunch. Maybe we could find them before it got too late.

We walked along an old fenceline on our way there, hoping maybe to find a stray bunch that I didn't know about. The little bit of ice and snow that had thawed down in the valley near the hills was now beginning to freeze again and we hadn't found anything yet. Looking back toward the truck, I wondered if it was wise to go farther, but only about another quarter of a mile lay between us and the pond where my friend and I had found some birds.

The little dog had gone ahead and was out of sight over a little rise. I moved another hundred yards, and when I saw him, he still hadn't found any birds.

While I was standing on the higher ground, I looked up at the hillside where there were a few scattered bushes and grass. Water seeped out of these ridges most of the time, but now everything was frozen because of the bitter north wind. Then something about four hundred yards away caught my eye. It was near the pond. In the darkening light from the overcast skies, I was unable to make out what it was. I assumed it must be a cow's head sticking up out of a little bunch of tall grass growing near the pond.

I moved a little farther south and a little in the direction of the pond, stopping occasionally to watch the pup work. The little valley seemed so quiet; I hadn't heard another hunter shoot the whole evening. I figured that the other gunners had had better sense than to be out on such a cold day. Once more, I moved another hundred yards in the general direction of the pond, until I was again standing on a little rise. Once more, the odd object caught my eye. This time, because I was closer, I could see that it was a dog and that it seemed to be standing still and looking at something on the ground.

I looked around for other hunters but saw no one. As I moved closer, the old dog still stood in the same place. I could see that he was a setter. He seemed very tired, but he continued to look straight ahead. His head seemed to be too big for his frail body. When I got closer, I saw that ice had formed on his undercoat and that his ribs stood out clearly. The long, shaggy tail swept back and forth like a pendulum. Its movement never ceased while I stood there, twenty yards away. It dawned on me that he was very old; far past his prime. The once-bright eyes were sunken and clouded, and I guessed that he had gone deaf from old age and too many shotgun blasts over his head. He didn't even know I was there. Once more I searched the landscape for someone who might be with him, but again there was no one.

I had already decided that the old dog was on birds--if not, he sure thought that he was. I had forgotten about my pup while I'd been studying the old dog. When I looked up, I could see him standing twenty yards behind the old dog. He was honoring that old-timer's point with everything he could stretch out.

The old dog was locked up and sensed nothing but the birds. Yet when I moved to within five steps of him, those dim eyes caught sight of me for the first time and he seemed startled. He looked up at my face just for an instant and I caught a message that only a hunter and an old dog can possibly understand. Immediately, the nose shot forward and the tail that had been moving straightened. No dog ever looked more beautiful and, as I moved forward a few feet to the place where the dog was looking, I felt sorry for him.

When ten or twelve quail lifted into the air, I knew I had to shoot one or two for the old setter. I got a straightaway and folded one that went to my right.

The old dog picked up the first bird and started toward me, but when he got within ten yards, he slowly put the bird down, his eyes seeming to say that he didn't know how much he could trust people anymore.

The pup had picked up the second bird and was nudging me with it. I took it and he fetched the one that the old dog had put down. Then he came to get his pat on the head. Dogs seem to greatly appreciate just a pat on the head.

As I stood and reloaded my gun, I looked around to see where the old dog was. I had no idea where the other birds had gone. I stood there in that late evening cold and wondered if all this had really happened. I felt inside my game pocket and there were two birds there, still warm, to tell me that it was all real.

I moved farther up the hill and looked in every direction. Finally, I saw the old dog crossing the slope above me. He moved as though his back legs were hobbled. He pulled them along behind him and I could tell that every step was extremely difficult, but he never gave in to his misery. The last I saw of him, he was headed south. I called to him but he kept going. Of course he couldn't hear me, but it seemed that I had to do something. I tried to catch up with him, but it was if he sensed my actions somehow and maybe remembered some past betrayal by a man.

I started toward the truck and realized that I felt obligated to find someone who knew about the old dog. There were only two or three houses within about two miles of where we were, and as far as I knew, none of those people kept bird dogs.

While I hurriedly loaded my pup in the dog box, I decided to drive the roads in that area and look for someone who had lost the old dog. Maybe he would be parked somewhere waiting for the dog to come back. But I found no one on the roads, and I couldn't find any signs of a place where anyone had parked and let a dog out. Then I thought of the only other place where anyone stayed. It was a pipeline shop about one mile east of where I had last seen the old dog.

I parked in front of the shop and went in just as they were about to leave for home. I asked them if they had ever seen an old setter bird dog around the place. To my surprise, they said yes. An old dog stayed around the shop sometimes. They said that some fellow had brought him out there, knowing that they liked to hunt some and maybe would take the dog. The dog had gotten too old and wasn't much use anymore; he just wandered the countryside and came back to the shop for a little feed when he needed it.

The old dog's plight kept me awake that night. I could still see the greatness come alive in him again when I walked up to his side. He may have been old and crippled, eyesight nearly gone and completely deaf, but no dog that ever breathed showed more greatness than that old setter did on that cold winter evening. I'm not sure I will ever be the same after seeing him.

When I told the men at the shop about the old dog that I had found on point, they asked if he had been onto anything. I took the birds from my coat and put them on the floor before them.

"Here's a present from the old dog," I said.

I suspect that they were the last birds ever taken over him.

10

WHY I TAUGHT MY BOYS TO BE HUNTERS

By Archibald Rutledge

Probably more than any other activity, fathers want their sons to be hunters. Fathers prepare for this from the moment their first child is born, and it makes no difference whether it's a son or daughter. The plans are the same. Teach them to handle a gun, teach them to shoot, buy that first license, pick out the first gun and on and on. Why do hunters and fathers feel this way? Is it because they want companions? That's part of it, but there's much more than that. We know that hunting is good for the mind, heart and body. A friend once told me that he hunts because he senses a true sense of freedom in the woods that he can find nowhere else in our hectic world. Rutledge wrote this story 55 years ago and his reasoning makes even more sense today. If you're a father with sons and daughters, perhaps Rutledge has found the words you've been looking for all these years.

I have said that my hunting has often been solitary; but that was chiefly in the early days. During the last twenty-five years I have rarely taken to the woods and fields in the shooting season without having one or more of my own sons with me. Few human relationships are closer than those established by a mutual contact with nature; and it has always seemed to me that if more fathers were woodsmen, and would teach their sons to be likewise, most of the so-called father-and-son problems would vanish.

Providence gave me three sons, only about a year and a half apart; and since it was not possible for me to give them what we usually call the advantages of wealth, I made up my mind to do my best by them. I decided primarily to make them sportsmen, for I have a conviction that to be a sportsman is a mighty long step in the direction of being a man. I thought also that if a man brings up his sons to be hunters, they will never grow away from him. Rather the passing years will only bring them closer, with a thousand happy memories of the woods and fields. Again, a hunter never sits around home forlornly, not knowing what in the world to do with his leisure. His interest in nature will be such that he can delight in every season, and he has resources within himself that will make life always seem worth while.

Hunters should be started early. As each one of my boys reached the age of six I gave him a single-shot .22 rifle, and I began to let him go afield with me. For a year or so I never let him load the gun, even with dust shot; but I just tried to give him some notions of how to handle it, of how to cross a ditch or a fence with it, and in what direction to keep the muzzle pointed.

It was a great day for each youngster when he shot his first English sparrow with a .22 shot shell.

From the time when the first one was six years old, I could never get into my hunting clothes without hearing, "Dad, take me along!" Sometimes an argument was added: "I will shoot straight. I will put it on him!" To these winning pleas I have always tried to give an affirmative answer, even when I had to alternate carrying a played-out boy and a played-out puppy. But I knew that I was on the right track when I was trying to impress on the younger generation the importance of shooting straight. I directly applied to my own children that old copy-book maxim, "Teach the young idea how to shoot." I think the rod and gun better for boys than the saxophone and the fudge sundae. In the first place, there is something inherently manly and home-bred and truly American in that expression, "shooting straight." The hunter learns that reward comes from hard work; he learns from dealing with nature that a man must have a deep respect for the great natural laws. He learns also, I think, in a far higher degree than any form of standardized amateur athletics can give him, to play the game fairly.

Most of our harmless and genuine joys in this life are those which find their source in primitive instincts. A man who follows his natural inclinations, with due deference to common sense and moderation, is usually on the right track. Now the sport of hunting is one of the most honorable of the primeval instincts of man. What human thrill is there in lounging into a grimy butcher-shop and sorrowfully surrendering a hard-earned simoleon for a dubious slab of inert beef? Certainly any true man would far rather trudge fifteen miles in inclement weather just for a chance at a grouse. Even if he gets nothing, he will be a younger and better man when he gets home, and with memories that will lighten the burden of the days when he cannot go afield.

A lot of good people, seeing me rearing my sons to be woodsmen, have offered me advice. "How can you love nature and yet shoot a deer?" "How can you bear to teach those children to kill things?"

These parlor naturalists and lollipop sentimentalists, whose knowledge of nature is such that they would probably take a flying buttress for a lovely game bird, are incapable of understanding that it is far less cruel to kill a wild deer than it is to poleax a defenseless ox in a stall. The ox has no chance; but the deer has about four chances out of five against even the good hunter. Besides, I have a philosophy which teaches me that certain game birds and animals are apparently made to be hunted, because of their peculiar food value and because their character lends zest to the pursuit of them. It has never seemed to me to be too far-fetched to suppose that Providence placed game here for a special purpose.

Hunting is not incompatible with the deepest and most genuine love of nature. Audubon was something of a hunter; so was the famous Bachman; so were both John Muir and John Burroughs. It has always seemed to me that any man is a better man for being a hunter. This sport confers a certain constant alertness, and develops a certain ruggedness of character that, in these days of too much civilization, is refreshing; moreover, it allies us to the pioneer past. In a deep sense, this great land of ours was won for us by hunters.

Again, there is a comradeship among hunters that has always seemed to me one of the finest human relationships. When fellow sportsmen meet in the woods or fields or the lonely marshes, they meet as friends who understand each other. There is a fine democracy about all this that is a mighty wholesome thing for young people to know. As much as I do anything else in life I treasure my comradeships with old, grizzled woodsmen. Hunting alone could have made us friends. And I want my boys to go through life making these humble contacts and learning from fellow human beings, many of them very unpretentious and simple-hearted, some of the ancient lore of nature that is one of the very finest heritages of our race. Nature always solves her own problems; and we can go far toward solving our own if we will listen to her teachings and consort with those who love her.

In the case of my own boys, from the .22 rifle they graduated to the .410 shotgun; then to a 20-gauge; then a 16; then a 12. I was guide for my oldest son, Arch, when he shot his first stag. We stalked him at sundown on Bull's Island, in the great sea-marsh of that magnificent preserve, creeping through the bulrushes and the myrtle bushes until we got in a position for a shot. And that night at the clubhouse, when I went to bed late, I found my young hunter still wide awake, no doubt going over our whole campaign of that memorable afternoon.

I was near my second son, Middleton, when he shot his first five stags. I saw all of them fall--and these deeds were done before he was eighteen.

I followed the blood-trail of the first buck my youngest son, Irvine, shot. He had let drive one barrel of his 16-gauge at this great stag in a dense pine thicket. The buck made a right-about face and headed for the river, a mile away. He was running with a doe, and she went on across the water. The buck must have known that he could not make it, for he turned up the plantation avenue, actually jumped the gate, splashing it with blood, and fell dead under a giant live-oak only eighty yards from the house!

It's one thing to kill a deer, and it's another to kill one and then have him accommodate you by running out of the wilds right up to your front steps. That kind of performance saves a lot of toting. This stag was an old swamp buck with massive antlers. Last Christmas my eldest son had only three days' vacation; but he got two bucks.

Yes, I have brought up my three boys to be hunters; and I know full well that when the wild creatures need no longer have any apprehensions about me, my grandchildren will be hard on their trail, pursuing with keen enjoyment and wholesome passion the sport of kings. While other boys are whirling in the latest jazz or telling dubious stories on street corners, I'd like to think that mine are deep in the lonely woods, far in the silent hills, listening to another kind of music, learning a different kind of lore.

This privilege of hunting is about as fine a heritage as we have, and it needs to be passed on unsullied from father to son. There is still hope for the race when some members of it are not wholly dependent upon effete and urbane artificialities for their recreation. A true hunter will never feel at home in a night club. The whole things would seem to him rather pathetic and comical--somehow not in the same world with solitary fragrant woods, rushing rivers and the elegant high-born creatures of nature with which he is familiar. Hunting gives a man a sense of balance, a sanity, a comprehension of the true values of life that make vicious and crazily stimulated joy a repellent thing.

I well remember the morning when I took all three of my boys on a hunt for the first time. I had told them the night before that we were going for grouse and had to make an early start for Path Valley. There must have been a romantic appeal in the phrase "early start," for I could hardly get them to sleep that night. And such a time we had getting all the guns and shells and hunting clothes ready, and a lunch packed, and the alarm clock set! And now, nine years after that memorable day, we still delight in making early starts together.

That day, before we had been in the dewy fringes of the mountain a half hour, as we were walking abreast about fifty yards apart, we had the good fortune to flush a covey of five ruffed grouse. It was the first time that any of my boys had had a shot at this grand bird, which to my way of thinking outpoints every other game bird in the whole world, bar none. An old cock with a heavy ruff fell to Middleton's gun. A young cock tried to get back over Irvine's head. It was a gallant gesture, but the little huntsman's aim was true, and down came the prince of the woodland.

Arch and I were a little out of range for a shot on the rise, but ere long we flushed other birds, and I had the satisfaction of seeing him roll his first *Bonasa umbellus*. We were walking through some second growth, which was fairly thick. I had just been telling him that in such cover a grouse is mighty likely to go up pretty fast and steep to clear the tree-tops, where, for the tiniest fraction of a split second, it will seem to pause as it checks its rise and the direction of its flight, which is to take it like a scared projectile above the forest. I had been telling Arch that the best chance under such circumstances was usually offered just as the grouse got above the sprouts and seemed to hesitate.

I had just taken up my position in line when out of a tangle of fallen grape-vines that had been draping a clump of sumac bushes a regal grouse roared up in front of Arch. I could see the splendid bird streaking it for the sky and safety. At first I was afraid that Arch would shoot too soon, then that he would shoot too late; either one would be like not shooting at all. But just as the cock topped the trees and tilted himself downward the gun spoke, and the tilt continued, only steeper and without control. With a heavy thud the noble bird dropped within my sight on the tinted leaves of the autumnal forest floor.

Fellow-sportsmen will appreciate what I mean when I say that was a great day for me. When a father can see his boy follow and fairly kill our most wary and splendid game bird, I think the Old Man has a right to feel that his son's education is one to be proud of. I'd far rather have a son of mine able to climb a mountain and outwit the wary creatures of the wilderness than to be able to dance the Brazilian busybody.

When Arch was thirteen, I had him up at daybreak with me one morning in the wilds of the Tuscarora mountains. From the crest of the wooded ridge on which we were standing we could see over an immense gorge on either side and beyond them, far away over the rolling ridges, northward and southward. It was dawn of the first day, and there were many hunters in the mountains. The best chance at a turkey in that country at such a time is to take just such a stand and wait for one to fly over or perhaps to come walking warily up the slope of one of the leaf-strewn gullies. We had been standing together for about fifteen minutes and had heard some shooting to the northward of us, three ridges away, when I saw a great black shape coming toward us over the tree-tops.

"Here he comes, son!" I told my youthful huntsman. "Hold for his head when he gets almost over you."

Three minutes later my boy was down on the slope of the gorge, retrieving a 19-pound gobbler, as proud as a lad could be, and entitled to be proud. It was all he could do to toil up the hill with his prize.

Irvine shot his first turkey on our plantation in Carolina. He was on a deer-stand when this old tom came running to him through the huckleberries. The great bird stood almost as tall as he did.

Middleton killed his first under peculiar circumstances. We walked into a flock together, at daybreak, and they scattered in all directions, but were too drowsy to fly far. He wounded a splendid bird, and it alighted in a tall yellow pine about a hundred yards from us. There was not enough cover to enable him to creep up to it, and the morning was so very still that I was afraid his first step would scare the gobbler from his lofty perch.

"I know what to do," he whispered to me as I stood at a loss to know what to advise. "Don't you hear that old woodpecker hammering on that dead pine? Every time he begins to rap I'm going to take an easy, soft step forward. Perhaps I can get close enough."

"Go ahead," I told him, and stood watching this interesting stalk.

The woodpecker proved very accommodating, and every other minute hammered loudly on the sounding tree. Step by cautious step Middleton got nearer. At last he raised his gun, and at its report the gobbler reeled earthward. I thought the little piece of woodcraft very neatly executed.

If the sentimentalist were right, hunting would develop in men a cruelty of character. But I have found that it inculcates patience, demands discipline and iron nerve, and develops a serenity of spirit that makes for a long life and long love of life. And it is my fixed conviction that if a parent can give his children a passionate and wholesome devotion to the outdoors, the fact that he cannot leave each of them a fortune does not really matter so much. They will always enjoy life in its nobler aspects without money and without price. They will worship the Creator in his mighty works. And because they know and love the natural world, they will always feel at home in the wide, sweet habitations of the Ancient Mother.

11

BIRD DOGS NEVER DIE

By Charles B. Martin, Sr.

Outdoor Life, December 1981

I like gun-dog stories because dogs do all these great (and sometimes not so great) things in the woods and there's no one around to brag about them. If no one wrote dog stories, how would the rest of the world know about our dogs? But we know that not all dog tales are happy. "Bird Dogs Never Die" is a short, but powerful love story. It's impossible to read about Crip without getting glassy eyed and that's the way it should be.

The dark sky seemed to mirror my troubled soul that long-ago November day. Leaden clouds hung heavy as I slowly deepened and widened a grave. Each spadeful of dank, musty earth brought me closer to a moment I faced with mounting dread. The time had come to bury old Crip, an English setter that meant the world to me.

Only someone who has loved a pet can know the bond that exists between a boy and his dog. In this case that bond was especially strong. I was a hunter, and Crip was one of the final, tangible links that bound us to the memory of my Uncle Luther. Crip was the last dog Luther had owned.

As I paused a moment in my digging, my mind was flooded with nostalgia for those long-gone days when Luther, Dad, Crip, and I hunted mountain grouse and meadow-dwelling bobwhite quail. I recalled the reason we used the nickname Crip instead of his real name, Spot. A car had run him down when he was a pup, breaking many bones and dooming him to hobble through life on three legs.

This handicap was physical only. There was nothing crippled about his noble spirit or his burning desire to hunt. His inability to range as wide as healthy dogs seemed to intensify his desire to find any bird nearby. I'd seen him put many of the county's finest dogs to shame when it came to pointing birds. He was exceptionally good at finding quail and holding his point until his hunter would flush the birds. Nobody who hunted with old Crip could remember a time when he flushed a quail.

While tossing the last bits of clay from the grave, I was crushed with the realization that I would never hunt again with my uncle and old Crip. Luther had traded his double-barrel shotgun and hunting clothes for an M1 rifle and the olive drab of a World War II infantry soldier. Leaving behind his lovely young wife and baby daughter, he had marched out of our valley never to return. Less than a month after his departure we had read and reread the tear-stained telegram that told us Luther wasn't coming home. A white cross in a Belgian cemetery marks his place for eternity.

I remembered well what he had said to me when he left home: "Take care of Crip and take him hunting every chance you get."

So the years had flown and Crip had grown old and the guns of hatred had long since ceased. Their rumble faded, and the significant sounds of war could be heard--the silent but somehow deafening sounds of sorrow and mourning. How long till men shall learn that the way to peace is not through war?

With the grave completed, I walked to the barn where Crip was lying on his bed of hay. I picked up a rifle I had left leaning against a manger and softly called his name. He wagged his tail feebly and lifted his pain-racked body. We had tried every medical means we could find in an attempt to heal him, but all were to no avail. The only merciful thing we could do was to put him out of his misery.

My dad and aunt had discussed having him put to sleep by a veterinarian, but I couldn't tolerate the idea because I didn't want Crip to die in unfamiliar surroundings. Instead, I determined to end his suffering myself and decided the best way to do that would be let him think we were going hunting again. Soon we headed toward his grave.

As Crip followed me through the woods he knew so well, he made a valiant effort to hunt. Neither the weakness of his legs nor the pain he bore could dim the enthusiasm for guns and hunting. His was the most indomitable spirit I had ever known.

When we reached the mound of freshly dug clay, I kneeled and cradled his head in my lap. No longer was I the teenager who had volunteered with false bravado to do this thing. I was now a heartsick boy whose tears fell on that noble head in my arms.

A few minutes later those arms trembled as I slowly raised the gun. "Dear God," I prayed, "if I'm ever to make a perfect shot, please let it be this." And then old Crip was gone.

I had chosen his final resting place carefully. It was along a trail, up near a meadow we had hunted many times. It was a place where we had often paused to admire the grandeur of the hazy Blue Ridge Mountains stretching from horizon to horizon. I alone know of the place where old Crip turned again toward home. But I realized that the location of a grave is unimportant. The place to bury a dog is in its master's heart. Buried there, it never really dies.

That's where I keep the memory of old Crip. Sometimes when the mood is right, I hear his footsteps on the pathways of my mind. He still returns to me in dreams though the winds above his grave have been blowing for 30 years. When frosty nights have splashed the forest canopy with red and gold, the memory of old Crip still walks beside me.

The ability to remember and to relive the past is one of the greatest gifts bestowed on man.

Through it we can transcend time and even death. It also complements the deep human desire to be remembered. I hope someone I love will pause to think of me when I too have vanished in that labyrinth of ended days.

12

DE SHOOTINEST GENT'MAN

By Nash Buckingham

*Nash's most famous story has had a long and glorious career.
1916: First published in Casper Whitney's magazine, Recreation,
where the editor, Edward Cave, bought it for $75, a good fee at that
time for an unknown writer. 1927: Reprinted in the first combined
issue of Outdoor Life & Recreation. 1930: Used in the anthology,
Classics of the American Shooting Field, by John C. Phillips (president
of American Wildfowlers) and Dr. Hill; 150 copies signed by Phillips,
Hill and the artist Frank Benson. Between 1930 and 1934: Used in a
gunning anthology by Harry McGuire. [son of the owner of Outdoor
Life.] 1934: Derrydale edition of De Shootinest Gent'man. [950
copies.] 1941: Scribner's edition of the single story, De Shootinest
Gent'man. 1943: Putnam edition, De Shootinest Gent'man. 1961:
Nelson collection, De Shootinest Gent'man and Other Hunting Tales.
[260 copies signed; also regular edition.] In Wild Fowl Decoys, 1934,
Joel Barber mentions a Windward House edition of De Shootinest
Gent'man.*

*Few writers have had a story published when they were 36, used
again when they were 47, 50, about 52, 54, 61, 63, and 81. If "De
Shootinest Gent'man" is a true story--and who would doubt it any
more than the existence of Lady Luck and the Happy Hunting--then
Nash Buckingham has Horace to thank not only for his best title
(among some great ones) but for his immortality as a writer. It is by
this story that Nash is known to 80 percent of his readers, many of*

whom think subliminally of Nash, not Dr. Money, as "De Shootinest Gent'man."

Like other stories in that first Derrydale collection, this was written during a period in Nash's life when that rich flow of Buckingham narrative was bursting to pour out under the pressure of his prime gunning years in an environment stiff with game and abounding with opportunity to shoot. Nash being Nash, the story would have to open with Molly's goose stew recipe. Irma Buckingham Witt describes Horace's helpmeet, Molly, as "the original five-by-five, and, oh, how she could cook up vittles'!"

The club is Beaver Dam, identified by Horace's presence and by the "Han'werker" blind. "The Judge"--James M. Greer--was a charter member of Beaver Dam.

Horace, as Horace always does, approaches perfection. Old photographs show him medium in height, not heavy, with full mustache, dressed not in hunting clothes, other than a shooting coat, but always wearing a vest, frequently a long overcoat, almost invariably a felt hat. But to see him you need no picture other than Nash's words and Horace's mellifluous expressions.

If Uncle Tomism in this story--and it is there--is objectionable, try to view a parallel situation with a French Canadian or a Swedish guide who has a weakness for the bottle. Remember the time period in which this story was written.

The legendary Captain Harold Money turns up sporadically in shooters' conversations, especially in the East and South. Nash wrote the story in 1916, but according to his inscription on a photograph it took place in 1908. In a letter dated 1954, here is what Buckingham wrote about Harold Money:

Harold Money, younger son of an old and honored British family, came to this country with his father, Capt. E. C. Money, who produced the earliest smokeless powders. They were a wonderful pair. Harold first attracted attention by winning the famous Carteret Handicap at live birds in the East and went on to become a professional exhibition shot for the old Winchester Repeating Arms Co. For several years his rating headed many lists.

When the circuits closed he'd come here to Memphis during the winter to enjoy the duck-club life. If there was ever a better all-around game shot, plus unselfish, gentlemanly spirit that endeared him to all, I have yet to meet him. I shot with Harold for many years, until 1908, when he returned to England.

Brilliantly educated, he was as much at home in an Indian wicki-up as at the court of St. James. From Ceylon he rushed into World War I. Years later, he returned to America and was with Abercrombie & Fitch in New York. He married the widow of the late Douglas Franchot and they retired to a lovely home on the Severn near Annapolis. He contracted pneumonia in the Adirondack Mountains two years later and passed on.

Nash placed Harold Money's age at one year older than his own. The photograph in "De Shootinest Gent'man" shows him as suave, with dark hair, gray at the temples, mixed-gray mustache and heavy eyebrows, whimsical mouth, somewhat large British nose, a shooter's gray eyes, a cigarette in a hand that never worked, and an easy manner evident through the camera.

As God made ducks and Horace, here is the story that made Nash Buckingham.

Supper was a delicious memory. In the matter of a certain goose stew, Aunt Molly had fairly outdone herself. And we, in turn, had jolly well done her out of practically all the goose. It may not come amiss to explain frankly and above board the entire transaction with reference to said goose. Its breast had been deftly detached, lightly grilled and sliced into ordinary "mouth-size" portions. The remainder of the dismembered bird, back, limbs, and all parts of the first part thereunto pertaining, were put into an iron pot. Keeping company with the martyred fowl, in due proportion of culinary wizardry, were sundry bell peppers, two cans of mock turtle soup, diced roast pork, scrambled ham rinds, peas, potatoes, some corn and dried garden okra, shredded onions, and pretty much anything and everything that Molly had lying loose around her kitchen. This stew, served right royally, and attended by outriders of "cracklin' bread," was flanked by a man-at-arms in the form of a saucily flavored brown gravy. I recall a side dish of broiled teal and some country puddin' with ginger pour-over, but merely mention these in passing.

So the Judge and I, in rare good humor (I forgot to add that there had been a dusty bottle of the Judge's famous port), as becomes sportsmen blessed with a perfect day's imperfect duck shooting, had discussed each individual bird brought to bag, with reasons, pro and con, why an undeniably large quota had escaped uninjured. We bordered upon that indecisive moment when bedtime should be imminent, were it not for the delightful trouble of getting started in that direction. As I recollect it, ruminating upon our sumptuous repast, the Judge had just countered my remark that I had never gotten enough hot turkey hash and beaten biscuits, by stating decisively that his craving for smothered quail remained inviolate, when the door opened softly and in slid "Ho'ace!" He had come, following a custom of many years, to take final breakfast instructions before packing the embers in "Steamboat Bill," the stove, and dousing our glim.

Seeing upon the center table, twixt the Judge and me, a bottle and the unmistakable ingredients and tools of the formers' ironclad rule for a hunter's nightcap, Ho'ace paused in embarrassed hesitation and seated himself quickly upon an empty shell case. His attitude was a cross between that of a timid gazelle scenting danger and a wary hunter sighting game and effacing himself gently from the landscape.

Long experience in the imperative issue of securing an invitation to "get his'n" had taught Ho'ace that it were ever best to appear humbly disinterested and thoroughly foreign to the subject until negotiations, if need be even much later, were opened with him directly or indirectly. With old-time members he steered along the above lines. But with newer ones or their uninitiated guests, he believed in quicker campaigning, or, conditions warranting, higher-pressure sales methods. The Judge, reaching for the sugar bowl, mixed his sweetening water with adroit twirl and careful scrutiny as to texture; fastening upon Ho'ace meanwhile a melting look of liquid mercy. In a twinkling, however, his humor changed and Ho'ace found himself in the glare of a forbidding menace, creditable in his palmiest days to Mister Chief Justice himself.

"Ho'ace," demanded the Judge, tilting into his now ready receptacle a gurgling, man's-size libation, "who is the best shot--the best duck shot--you have ever paddled on this lake--barring--of course, a-h-e-m-m--myself?" Surveying himself with the coyness of a juvenile, the Judge stirred his now beading toddy dreamily, and awaited the encore. Ho'ace squirmed a bit as the closing words of the Judge's query struck home with appalling menace upon his ear. He plucked nervously at his battered headpiece. His eyes, exhibiting a vast expanse of white, roamed pictured walls and smoke-dimmed ceiling in furtive, reflective, helpless quandary. Then, speaking slowly and gradually warming to his subject, he fashioned the following alibi.

"Jedge, y' know, such, us all has ouh good an' ouh bad days wid de ducks. Yes, my lawdy, us sho' do. Dey's times whin de ducks flies all ovah ev'ything an' ev'ybody, an' still us kain't none o' us hit nuthin' - lak me an' you wuz' dis mawnin', Jedge, down in de souf end trails." At this juncture the Judge interrupted, reminding Ho'ace severely that he meant when the Judge--not the Judge and Ho'ace--was shooting.

"An' den dey's times whin h'it look lak dey ain't no shot too hard nur nary duck too far not t' be kilt. But Mistah Buckin'ham yonder--Mistah Nash he brung down de shootin'est gent'man whut took all de cake. H'its lots o' de member he'ah whuts darin' shooters, but dat fren' o' Mistah Nash's--uummp-uummpphh--doan nevuh talk t' me 'bout him whur de ducks kin' hear, 'cause dey'll leave de laik ef dey known he's even comin' dis way.

"Dat gent'man rode me jes' lak he wax er saddle an' he done had on rooster spurs. Mistah Nash he brung him on down he'ah an' say" `Ho'ace,' he say, `he'ahs a gent'man from Englan',' he say, `Mistah Money--Mistah Horl' Money,'--an' say, `I wants you t' paddle him t'morrow an' see dat hi gits er gran' shoot--unnerstan'?' I say--`Yaas, suh, Mistah Nash,' I say, `dat I'll sho'ly do, suh. Mistah Money gwi' hav' er fine picnic ef I has t' see dat he do m'se'f--but kin he shoot, suh?'

"`Mistah Nash,' he say, `Uh-why-uh-yaas, Ho'ace, Mistah Money he's uh ve'y fair shot--'bout lak Mistah Immit Joyners or Mistah Hal Howard.' I say t' m'se'f, I say, `Uummmpphh--huummpphh w-e-e-l-l he'ah now, ef dats de case me an' Mistah Money gwi' do some shooting' in de mawnin.'"

"Mistah Money he talk so kin'er queer an' brief lak, dat I hadda' pay mighty clos't inspection t'whut he all de time a-sayin'. But nex' mawnin', whin me an' him goes out in de bote, I seen he had a gre't big ol' happy bottle o' Brooklyn Handicap in dat shell box so I say t' m'se'f, I say, `W-e-l-l-l, me an' Mistah Money gwi' git erlong someway, us is.'

"I paddles him on up de laik an' he say t' me, say, `Hawrice-uh--hav' yo'-er-got any wager,' he say, `or proposition t' mek t' me, as regards,' he say, `t' shootin' dem dar eloosive wil' fowls?' he say."

"I kinder studies a minit, 'cause lak I done say, he talk so brief, den I says, `I guess you is right 'bout dat, suh.'

"He say, `Does you follow me, Hawrice, or is I alone?' he say.

"I says, `Naw, suh, Boss, I leaves all dat wid you, suh, trustin' t' yo' gin'rosity, suh.'

"Ve'y good, Hawrice,' he say. `I sees you doan' grasp de principul. Now I will mek you de proposition,' he say. I jus' kep' on paddlin'. He say--`Ev'y time I miss er duck you gits er dram frum dis he'ah bottle--ev'y time I kills a duck, I gits de drink--which is h'it?--Come--come--speak up, my man.'

"I didn' b'lieve I done heard Mistah Money rightly an' I says--`Uh--Mistah Money,' I says, `suh, does you mean dat I kin hav' de chice whedder you misses or kills ev'y time an' gits er drink?'

"He say--Dat's my defi,' he say.

"I says--`Well, den--w-e-l-l--den, ef dats de case, I gwi', I gwi' choose ev'y time yo' misses, suh.' Den i say t' m'se'f, I say, Ho'ace, right he'ah whar you gotta be keerful, 'ginst you fall outa de bote an' git fired frum de Lodge; cause ef'n you gits er drink ev'ytime dis gent'man misses an' he shoot lak Mister Hal Howard, you an' him sho gwi' drink er worl' o' liquah--er worl' o' liquah.'

"I pushes on up nur'ly to de Han'werker stan', an I peeks in back by da' l'il pocket whut shallers offn de laik, an' I sees some sev'ul blackjacks--four of 'em--settin' in dar. Dey done seen us, too. An' up come dey haids. I spy 'em twis'in an' turnin'--gittin' raidy t' pull dey freight frum dere. I says, `Mistah Money,'' I say, `yawnder sets some ducks--look out now, suh, 'cause dey gwi' try t' rush on out pas' us whin dey come outa dat pocket.' Den I think--`W-e-l-l-l, he'ah whar I knocks de gol' fillin' outa de mouf o' Mistah Money's bottle o' Brooklyn Handicap!'

"I raised de lid o' de shell box an' dar laid dat ol' bottle--still dar. I say, `Uuuuummmpp-huuummpph.' Jus' 'bout dat time up goes dem black-haids an' outa dar dey come--dey did--flyin' low to de watah--an' sorter raisin' lak--y' knows how dey does h'it, Jedge?

"Mistah Money he jus' pick up dat fas' feedin' gun--t'war er pump--not one o' dese he'ah afromatics--an' whin he did, I done reach fo' de bottle, 'cause I jes' natcherly knowed dat my time had come. Mistah Money he swing down on dem bullies--Ker-py-ker-py--powie-powie--slamp-slamp-slamp--ker-splash--Lawdy mussy--gent'mens, fo' times, right in de same place h'it sounded lak--an de las' duck fell ker-flop--almos' in ouh bote.

"I done let go de bottle, an' Mistah Money say--mightly cool lak--say, `Hawrice,' he say, `kin'ly to examin' dat las' chap clos'ly,' he say, `an obsurve,' he say, 'efn he ain' shot thru de eye.'

"I rakes in dat blackjack, an' sho' nuff--bofe eyes done shot plum out--yaas, suh, bofe of 'em right on out. Mistah Money say, `I wuz--er--slightly afraid,' he say, `dat I had done unknowin'ly struck dat fellah er trifle too far t' win'ward,' he say. `A ve'y fair start, Hawrice,' he say. `You'd bettah place me in my station, so that we may continue on wid'out interruption,' he say.

"`Yaas, suh,' I say, `I'm on my way right dar now, suh,' an' I say to m'se'f, I say, `Mek haste an' put dis gent'man in his bline an' give him er proper chanc't to miss er duck.' I didn' hones'ly b'lieve but whut killin' all four o' dem other ducks so peart lak wuz er sorter accident. So I put him on de Han'werker bline. He seen I kep' de main shell bucket an' de liquah, but he never said nuthin'. I put out de m'coys an' den cre'p back wid' de bote into de willers t' watch.

"Pretty soon, he'ah come er ole drake flyin' mighty high. Ouh ole hen bird she holler t' him, an' de drake he sorter twis' his haid an' look down. I warn't figurin' nuthin' but whut Mistah Money gwi' let dat drake circle an' come 'mongst de m'coys--but aw! aw! All uv'er sudden he jus' raise up sharp lak an'--Ker-powie! Dat ole drake jus' throw his haid onto his back an' ride on down--looked t' me lak he fell er mile--an' whin he hit he throw'd watah fo' feet! Mistah Money he nuvver said er word--jus' sot dar!

"He'ah come another drake--way off to de lef'--up over back o' me. He turn 'roun--quick lak--he did--an' ker-zowies--he cut him on down, too. Dat drake fall way back in de willers an' co'se I hadda wade after 'im.

"Whil'st I wuz gone, Mistah Money shoot twice--an' whin I come stumblin' back, dar laid two mo' ducks wid dey feets in de air. Befo' I hav' time t' git in de bote agin he done knock down er hen away off in de elbow brush.

"I say, `Mistah Money, suh, I hav' hunted behin' som' far-knockin' guns in my time, an' I'se willin, sho--but ef you doan, please suh, kill dem ducks closer lak, you gwi' kill yo' Ho'ace in de mud.' He say--`Da's all right 'bout dat,' he say, `go git de bird--he kain't git er-way 'cause h't's daid as er wedge.'

"Whin I crawls back to de bote dat las' time--it done got mighty col'. Dar us set--me in one en' a-shiverin' an' dat ole big bottle wid de gol' haid in de far en'. Might jus' ez well bin ten miles so far ez my chances had done gone.

"Five mo' ducks come in--three singles an' er pair o' sprigs. An' Mistah Money he chewed 'em all up lak good eatin'. One tim, tho'--he had t' shoot one o' them high-flyin' sprigs twice, an' I done got halfway in de bote--reachin' fer dat bottle--but de las' shot got 'im. Aftah while, Mistah Money say, `Hawrice,' he say, `how is you hittin' off--my man?'

"Mistah Money,' I say, `I'se pow'ful col', suh, an' ef yo' wants me t' tell you de trufe, suh, I b'lieves I done made er pow'ful po' bet.' He say, `Possibly so, Hawrice, poss'bly so.' But dat `poss'bly' didn't get me nuthin'.

"Jedge, y' Honor, you know dat gent'man sot dar an' kill ev'ry duck whut come in, an' had his limit long befo' de eight o'clock train runned. I done gone t' watchin', an' de las' duck whut come by wuz one o' dem lightnin' express teals. He'ah he come--look lak somebody done blowed er buckshot pas' us. I riz' up an' hollered-- `Fly fas' ole teal, do yo' bes'--'caus' Ho'ace need er drink.' But Mistah Money just jumped up an' throw'd him fo'ty feet--skippin' 'long de watah. I say, `Hol' on, Mistah Money, hol' on--you don' kilt de limit.'

"`Oh!' he say, `I hav'--hav' I?'

"I say, `Yaas, suh, an' you ain' bin long 'bout h'it, neither!'

"He say, `Whut are you doin' gittin so col', den?'

"I say, `I spec' findin; out dat I hav' done made er bad bet had er lot t' do wid de air.'

"An' dar laid dat Brooklyn Handicap all dat time--he never touched none--an' me neither. I paddles him on back to de house, an' he come a-stalkin' on in he'ah, he did--lookin' kinda mad lak-- never said nuthin' 'bout no drink. Finally, he say, `Hawrice,' he say, `git me a bucket o' col' watah.' I say t' m'se'f, I say, `W-e-l-ll--dat mo' lak h'it--ef he want er bucket o' watah--you gwi' see some drinkin' now.'

"Whin I come in wid de pail, Mistah Money took offin all his clo'es an' step out onto de side po'ch an say, `Th'ow dat watah ovah me, Hawrice, I am lit'rully compel,' he say, `t' have my col' tub ev'ry mawnin'.' M-a-n-n-n! I sho' thow'd dat ice col' watah onto him wid all my heart an' soul. But he jus' gasp an' hollah, an' jump up an' down an' slap hisse'f. Den he had me rub him red wid er big rough towel. I sho' rubbed him, too. Come in one de clubroom he'ah, he did, an' mek hisse'f comfort'ble in dat big rockin' chair yonder--an' went t' readin. I brought in his shell bucket an' begin' cleanin' his gun. But I see him kinder smilin' t' hisse'f. Atta while, he says, `Hawrice,' he say, `you hav' los' you' bet?'

"I kinda hang my haid lak, an' 'low, `Yaas, suh, Mistah Money, I don' said farewell to de liquah!'

"He say, `Yo' admits, den, dat you hav' don' los' fair an' squar'--an' dat yo' realizes h'it?'

"`Yaas, suh!'

"He say, `Yo' judgmint,' he say, `wuz ve'y fair, considerin',' he say, 'de great law uv' av'ridge--but circumstances,' he say, `has done render de ult'mate outcome subjec' to de mighty whims o' chance?'

"I say, `Yaas, suh,'--ve'y mournful lak.

"He say, `In so far as realizin' on annything 'ceptin de mercy o' de Cote'--say--`you is absolutely hon-est--eh! may man?'

"I say, `Yaas, suh, barrin' yo' mercy, suh.'

"Den he think er moment, an' day, `Verree-verree--good!' Den he 'low, `Since you acknowledge de cawn, an' admits dat you hav' done got grabbed,' he say, `step up'--he say, an' git you a tumbler-- an po' yo'se'f er drink--po' er big one, too.'

"I nev'uh stopped f' nuthin' den--jes' runned an' got me er glass outa de kitchen. Ole Molly, she say, `Whur you goin' so fas'?' I say `Doan stop me now, ol' woman--I got business--an' I sho' poh'd me er big bait o' liquah--er whol' sloo' o' liquah. Mistah Money say, `Hawrice--de size o' yo' po'tion,' he say, `is primus facious ev'dence,' he say, `dat you gwi' spout er toas' in honor,' he say, `o' d' occasion.'

"I say, `Mistah Money, suh,' I say--`all I got t' say, suh, is dat you is de king-pin, champeen duck shooter so far as I hav' done bin

in dis life--an' ve'y prob'ly as fur ez I'se likely t' keep on goin', too.'
He sorter smile t' hisse'f!

"Now, suh, please, suh, tell me dis--is you evah missed er duck--
anywhar--anytime--anyhow--suh?'

"He say, `Really, Hawrice,' he say, `you embarrasses me,' he
say, `so hav' another snifter--there is mo', consider'bly mo',' he
say, `in yo' system, whut demands utt'rance.'

"I done poh'd me another slug o' Brooklyn Handicap, an' say--
`Mistah Money, does you expec' to' evah miss another duck ez long
ez you lives, suh?'

"He say, `Hawrice,' he say, `you embarrasses me,' he say,
`beyon' words--you ovahwhelms me,' he say--`git t' Hell outa
he'ah, befor' you gits us bofe drunk!'"

13

"DUCKS? YOU BAT YOU!"

By Gordon MacQuarrie

This is a duck-hunting story by Gordon MacQuarrie, the master of outdoor tales. We all know about duck hunting, perhaps the most uncomfortable form of gunning. Imagine standing for hours in a blind on a floor of ice or wading a shoreline where your knees break the ice. But we go back again and again, season after season, battering our bodies with wet, wind and bitter cold. Why? MacQuarrie says it better than I, but it's still difficult to explain what happens to us when you hear "Take 'em! Now!"

Tonight is the end of summer. A needle-fine rain is pelting the shingles. Autos swish by on wet concrete. Until now summer has been in full command. This full, cold rain is the first harbinger of autumn.

Maybe the cold rain started me off. A flood of recollections of my first duck-hunting trip crowds everything else from my mind. Just such a rain--only colder--was falling from northern Wisconsin skies that night in late October, many years ago, when the President of the Old Duck Hunters Association, Inc., rapped at my door.

It was an impatient rap. I found him standing in the hall, quizzical, eager, in his old brown mackinaw that later was to become his badge of office. As always, only a top button of the mackinaw was fastened. His brown felt hat dripped rain. Below the sagging corners of the mackinaw were high tan rubber boots. He danced a brief jig, partly to shake off the rain and partly to celebrate an impending duck hunt.

"Hurry up!" he said.

"Where?"

"You're going duck hunting."

That was news. I had never been duck hunting. Not once in a varied life devoted to fishing and hunting had I ever hunted ducks. For some reason, ducks had not appealed to me. They had just been something that flew over a lake where I was fishing late in the year. I didn't know it then, but I was much like a person who has grown to maturity without having read *Robinson Crusoe*.

"Shut the door!" a voice cried from within my house.

It was my wife, the daughter of the President, the only person who awes Mr. President. He shuffled through the door with alacrity and took a tongue-lashing for sprinkling water on the floor.

"Who's going duck hunting?" demanded the lady, adding, "and who says who can go duck hunting? Isn't it enough that he spends all his idle moments fishing?"

"It's like this," began Hizzoner. "I told him last summer that now, since he was more or less one of the family, I ought to take him duck hunting. He's been at our house eating ducks and currant jam for years. Why shouldn't he contribute to the--er--groaning board?"

"I see," said the daughter of the President cannily. "You want someone to row the boat!"

"I do not!" he replied indignantly. "I even borrowed a gun for him."

"You'll find he won't row. He won't even put up curtain rods. He looks like a dead loss for both of us."

"I'll take a chance on him."

From a closet she helped me resurrect heavy clothing, including an old sheepskin coat. When I was ready, the President advised his only heir that he would return the body safely some time the next evening. It was then about eight P.M. The lady whom I had wed only some four months previously sat down resignedly with a magazine. Her parting injunction was: "Mallards. Get some mallards."

A loaded car was at the curb. Wedged in a corner of the backseat beside duffel and a crate of live duck decoys was a huge figure that answered to the name of Fred. Later I was to learn that better duck shots have seldom displayed their wares on any of our local waters.

Down sandy Highway 35 with the rain streaking the windshield, off to the right at the store in Burnett County, over the humpbacked hills, then into a yard beyond with a light from a house gleamed among huge oak trees. As we drove up, a floodlight came on, as though someone within the house had been waiting for us.

It was Norm. Always there is a Norm for duck hunters who really mean it, some vigilant sentinel of the marshes who phones to say, "The flight is in." Norm was apprehensive. As we stored things in our allotted cabin we did not have to be reminded by him that it was growing colder. The rain was abating, and a northwest wind was rocking the oaks. "Little Bass may be frozen over," said Norm. "You should have come when I first phoned, two days ago. The temperature has fallen from fifty-five to forty since sunset."

We occupied the cabin. There were two full-sized beds. Norm built up a roaring jack-pine fire in the little airtight stove. There was much palaver along instructional lines for my benefit. Later my two benefactors prepared for bed.

"We'll give you the single bed," said the President magnanimously. "Fred and I are used to sleeping together. We'll put this extra blanket between the beds. Whoever gets cold and needs it can just reach over for it. Good night."

In five minutes they were asleep. Outside the wind rose. Even before I fell asleep, only half warm, I contemplated the probability of grabbing that blanket. Later I woke. I was somewhat congealed. I reached for the blanket. It was gone. I tried to fall asleep without it, but the cold was steadily growing worse.

Teeth chattering, I got up, lit a kerosene lamp and discovered the blanket carefully tucked around the two sleeping forms in the other bed. Sound asleep and snoring gently lay my two kind old friends. I wouldn't for the world snake that blanket off their aging bones. Not me!

I piled all available clothing on top my own thin blanket and tried again to sleep. At times I almost succeeded, but it was along toward 3:30 A.M. when I got up, lit a fire in the stove and thawed out. Then I dozed in an old rocking chair, to be awakened soon by a loud thumping on the single wall of the cabin.

It was Norm delivering the summons to his hunters. I turned up the wick on the lamp. The President and Fred awakened languorously. The President sat upright, threw his legs over the edge of the bed and studied the top of the table where the blanket had rested.

"Just looking for scratches in the varnish," he said. "Dreamed last night I heard someone reaching for that blanket. Wasn't you, was it? Surely a young man with your abounding vitality wouldn't be needing an extra blanket?"

"Why, we've got the blanket ourselves," chimed in Fred. "Now isn't that funny? Do you know, I had a dream too. Dreamed I was cold in the night and got up and took the derned blanket."

Since then I have learned to get that extra blanket in a hurry.

In Norm's kitchen there was a beaming platter of eggs and bacon. When it was empty, the platter was refilled with sour-cream pancakes, such as people often talk about but seldom can get. And after that a big white coffeepot was passed around as the Old Duck Hunters, Inc. washed down layer after layer of toast.

Outside it was bitter cold. The first really arctic blast had helped to dry the sand roads. Where it did not dry them the cold froze them, so that the car lurched and bumped along the ruts. There was the faintest hint of dawn as the car turned through a cornfield, plunged over rough ground a hundred yards and came to a stop near the base of a long point thrusting into the middle of a narrow, shallow lake.

This point on Little Bass Lake was--and still is--one of the most sought-after ducking points in northwest Wisconsin. Situated north of Big Yellow, this shallow lake with its swampy shores is a natural haven for ducks escaping bombardment on the bigger lake.

From a nearby patch of scrub oak the President hauled at something until, in the faint light, I saw he had hold of a duck boat. I helped him drag it to the water. He paddled off through thin ice inshore to spread the decoys in open water. While he was busy at this morning ritual the searing slash of duck wings came down to us a half dozen times. Fred called to him to hurry, but no one hurries the President when he is making a set.

Finally he came ashore and occupied the small scrub oak blind alongside mine. Even then he was not content to sit and wait, as was Fred in the nearby blind, but counted over and over again the wooden decoys. And was dissatisfied when he had 32. "Anyone knows you've got to have an uneven number. Why, thirteen is better than any even number!" he chafed.

I just sat. Said I to myself, "So this is duck hunting." Just sit and wait.

Then there was a searing roar in back of us. I was about to raise my head to see what it was, but the mittened hand of Mr. President seized my shoulder and pulled me down to the sand floor of the blind. He himself seemed to be groveling in the sand, and from the nearby cover where Fred skulked I heard him stage-whisper: "Don't move. They're flying in back to look us over."

Twice again the sound of many wings cleaving the frosty air was borne down to us. At no time did I dare look up. The sound faded, disappeared entirely, then swelled again, louder and louder. When it seemed it could grow no louder, it changed to a hissing diminuendo. That sound was my first introduction to the music of stiff, set wings on a long glide down.

"Now!" Maybe it was Fred who said it, maybe it was Mr. President.

Before I had thrust my head over the parapet of scrub oak Fred's 32-inch double had sounded and the President, who shot a pump in those days, had fired once and was grunting and straining to operate the action for the next shot. He had to catch that old corn sheller of his just right to make it throw the empty out and a new shell in. Always, whether it worked smoothly or not, the President gave off a groaning, whining sound between shots, like an angry terrier held back from a square meal. He got off three shots before I could make out a low-flying squad of dark objects hightailing across the lake.

"Bluebills," said the President.

On the open water beyond the rushes and in the quieter water on the very thin ice were five objects. I dragged the duck boat from its thicket and retrieved them. One of them had green on its wings. "What the--?" said Fred. "Look, Al! One greenwing among those bluebills."

So this was duck hunting. Well, not bad. Not bad at all. Indeed not!

The sounds of swift wings and booming guns were good sounds. The smell of burned powder was a good smell. The feel of those birds, warm in a bare hand, was a good feeling. My toes had been cold; now they were tingling. I knew those five ducks would go best with wild rice and currant jelly. They made a nice little pile at our feet in the blind.

After a while Gus Blomberg, who owned the point and lived in a little house 500 yards back of us, came down through the oaks to see what was going on. He took a chew of snuff and said: "Halloo-o-o! How iss it, eh? Nice docks, you bat you!"

Great guy, Gus. Fred gave him a dollar. That was for the use of his point. Gus said "Tenk you," and also, "How 'bout leetle coffee at noon, eh? Goes good cold day. You bat you!"

Gus went away. The President stood up occasionally and beat his mitts together to warm his fingers. Fred just sat. He had enough fat to keep him warm. I never saw him wear gloves in a blind, even on frightfully cold December mornings. All Fred wore was his old shooting jacket and a cigarette. He could keep his cigarette lit in a cloudburst.

Other ducks came in. Some went on, and some stayed. After a while it occurred to me that I might try a shot at a duck myself.

"Haven't you had your gun here all this time?" asked the President. And he meant it; he had been too busy to think of anything but that early-morning flight. He took me back to the car and unearthed a short-barreled hammerlock, the fore piece of which was held firm by close-wrapped wire.

"It's the best I could find around the neighborhood," he said. "The choke has been sawed off. Don't shoot at anything unless it's on top of you."

So I had a gun. This duck-hunting business was getting better and better.

Back in the blind, Fred had a couple more down. A flock of four bluebills came in. They were trusting souls. They neither circled nor hesitated. They came spang in, from straight out in front, low. They set their wings. I picked out one and fired--both barrels. One fell at the second shot.

My first duck! Lying out there on the thin ice, white breast up, dead as a doornail. The President and Fred had declined to shoot. They were furthering the education of a novice. They were, in fact, letting the duck-hunting virus take full effect. They laughed at me and pounded me on the back and kidded me, and all day after that they seemed to get an awful kick out of just looking at me and grinning.

About noon it began to snow. The wind fell off. The decoys froze in tightly. Fred stirred and said, "Coffee!" Hizzoner explained to me that it was necessary to pull in the blocks before leaving the blind. I was glad for the exercise. After coffee and some of the other things had been duly consumed, we returned to the blind, Fred to his motionless waiting. Hizzoner to his quick, birdlike neck craning.

The President usually saw the ducks first and signaled Fred. It did not perturb Fred much. The only sign of excitement from him was a gradual drawing-in of his neck, turtlelike. Then he would stamp out the last quarter inch of his cigarette and wait. At the crucial moment he didn't stand to fire; he just straightened out his legs and sort of rared up. He was by far the best duck shot I have ever seen.

Maybe I killed another duck; I am not sure. From then on I shot with the others. They had let me have my chance. I had killed a duck. It had been an easy shot. They knew that. So did I. But they did not speak of it. They just kept grinning, for they must have known I had been ordained to love the game and they were glad to help a natural destiny work itself out.

They grinned when I threw myself into the small chores that beset the duck hunter. Dragging the duck boat from the thicket for a pickup, cutting new boughs for the blind, walking around the sedgy shore of Little Bass to pick up a cripple that had drifted over, driving back for a pack of cigarettes for Fred.

To all these tasks I set myself eagerly. They came as part of the game. Those two rascals had frozen me the night before; but they had introduced me to something new and something good, and I was grateful.

Since then, while hunting with these two I have felt this obligation to do my part. Both are many years older than I, and they have appreciated it, but, of course, never mentioned it. They would prefer to guy me with mild rebuke, criticize my shooting and otherwise continue the good work already well begun.

Of such stuff are the recollections of that first ducking trip. Diverse images, grateful peeks back at two wise and capable practitioners of what has become for me the most dramatic thing in outdoor sports.

The outdoors holds many things of keen delight. A deer flashing across a burn, a squirrel corkscrewing up a tree trunk, a sharptail throbbing up from the stubble--all these have their place in my scheme of things. But the magic visitation of ducks from the sky to a set of bobbing blocks holds more of beauty and heart-pounding thrill than I have ever experienced afield with rod or gun. Not even the sure, hard pluck of a hard-to-fool brown trout, or the lurching smash of a river smallmouth has stirred me as has the circling caution of ducks coming to decoys.

The afternoon wore on. Shortly before quitting time Gus came back, to stand with Fred for a chance at a few mallards. He took a brace and was satisfied. Mr. President said he thought he'd take a walk around the north end of Little Bass "just for the fun of it." Gus said he might find a mallard or two if there was open water, "but you got to sneak opp on dem. You bat!"

"You bat you, too, Gus," said the President. He buttoned the second button on the brown mackinaw and headed into the swirling flakes.

Fred lit a cigarette. We waited. Collars and mittens were now soggy with snow water. Fred's magic cigarette somehow managed to stay lit and in the waning light glowed more brightly. From the north end of the lake came four reports, muffled by the distance and the snow.

"Ay hope iss dem mollard," said Gus. "Al, he like dem mollard, you bat you!"

We were picked up and packed up when the President returned. The President had two mallards, of course. He dropped them in the car trunk with the other birds and unbuttoned the top button of the old brown mackinaw. We stood in the snow and said good-bye to Gus. Added to his brace of birds were three more that Fred gave him. He turned and walked away through the rasping cornstalks with a final, "You bat you!"

The President addressed me: "How'd you like it?"

In those days I was very young. It took me a long time to try to say what I felt. I have never succeeded yet. I simply babbled.

We drove out of the cornfield, stopped to yell good-bye to Norm, who came out to his back door to wave, and then headed for the main highway. I drove. Fred reposed in the back, comfortable as the clucking ducks against whose crate he leaned. At my side sat the President. The light from the cowl partly illuminated his strong, sharp features.

Finally I said: "Wish you had let me in on this earlier in the season. There won't be another duck weekend after today."

The President flicked cigar ashes and replied: "I thought of that, but decided to break it to you gently. Too much of a good thing is bad for a growing boy."

14

THE GREAT JONESBORO
PIGEON SHOOT

By Jim Carmichel

Outdoor Life, March 1980

Whenever a fast gun shows up in town, there's always some young kid who will try to make a name for himself by goading an old gunfighter into a shootout in front of a saloon. In Jim Carmichel's case, it wasn't a young kid...it was pigeons defecating with reckless abandon. And it wasn't in front of a saloon...it was the town courthouse. Carmichel, Outdoor Life's shooting editor, had a reputation to uphold. Did he do it? You be the judge!

T he whole thing got started when Bob Jenkins' second-oldest daughter was accused of shoplifting a brassiere at Modene and Mabel's Discount Variety Store.

Bob (whose full name is Robert E. Lee Jenkins), like most folks who live on the lower end of Washington County, took his daughter's troubles to Fry (for Friedman L.) Bacon, a lawyer of some local repute. Fry Bacon is one of the last of that dwindling species of attorneys once admitted to the bar after a period of having "read law," but with no other formal training. This shortcoming has been of no noticeable difficulty to Fry Bacon, who describes himself as a champion of poor people's causes, and in return for legal services, has been known to take chickens, coon hounds and enough odd parcels of land to make him the county's biggest property owner.

Not one to let textbook law interfere with a good courtroom battle, Fry Bacon's favorite tactic is to open his Bible to some random page, wave it in the faces of judge and jury, shout that there is no higher law than the law of God, then have the jury get down on its collective knees while he leads the jurors in prayer for his dear misguided client, who has just recently been washed in the blood of the lamb and aims to spend the rest of his life doing kind deeds and "helping out widder women."

Fry Bacon was just the man to represent Robert E. Lee Jenkins' daughter.

In Fry Bacon's opinion the theft of a brassiere was a rather delicate subject and hardly one to be discussed before a courtroom audience. The word "brassiere" was abhorrent to him under such circumstances, as was the diminutive form "bra," so he substituted "set of briars," thumping his fists to his chest to indicate their approximate purpose and his own apparent meaning.

The case did not go well for Fry Bacon. His assertion that the poor girl was feeble-minded did not produce the desired effect, nor did his pleas that the lass was "with child" by a stranger last seen two years before. Seeing no hope in this line of defense, he turned to attack the two eye witnesses as "godless sinners and short-skirted harlots" and was just warming to this line when it happened.

Six tons of pigeon manure came cascading through the courtroom ceiling. It covered the jury, it covered the godless harlots, it covered Hizzoner the judge and it covered Fry Bacon. It covered them with six tons of dry, crusty, choking pigeon droppings that had been accumulating in the courthouse attic for decades, straining at the ceiling rafters and needing only the shock wave of Fry Bacon's rhetoric to set them free.

"Ladies and gentlemen of the jury," Fry Bacon is reputed to have said when the dust had cleared, "behold the wrath of the Lord."

The case was dismissed and the courthouse closed for six weeks because, as one Jonesboro wag put it, "The wheels of justice can't turn in that stuff."

The episode occurred not without some warning. About 15 years earlier, Bill Bowman, a leading Jonesboro humanitarian, had noted that the pigeons had so gummed up the courthouse clockworks that each hour was lasting about 80 minutes. The matter had been brought up at the City Council meeting, where Virgil Meeks suggested that the additional time was probably a good thing and the clock should not be tampered with. The Council agreed and voted 11 to 1 to leave the clock alone.

But the collapse of the courtroom ceiling meant something had to be done. The first order of business was to clear out the mess, and that in itself brought about a political scandal which almost brought down the county government. The lowest bid to haul away the pigeon manure ran into some thousands of dollars, enough to cause a countywide financial crisis, but at the last minute Mort Screeb, who owned a tomato farm down by the Chucky River, stepped in and said that the stuff was great tomato fertilizer and that he would haul it off for nothing. His one condition, however, was that he be allowed to take it as he needed it, which, questioning disclosed, might cover three or four years. In the end a cleanup crew was hired to cart it off, but the ensuing political fight, with Screeb screaming kickback, produced a shakeup in Washington County politics which continues even to this day.

Despite all the uproar a few cool heads noted that nothing was being done about the pigeons. They were as happy as ever, perching on the belfry railings, roosting in the clockworks, building more nests, hatching chicks and contributing hourly to another avalanche.

The county's first step was to hire professional exterminators. They rigged a cannonlike affair which made a burping noise guaranteed to frighten pigeons and starlings and other winged creatures. The Jonesboro pigeons loved it. It would burp and they would coo, and in winter they warmed their feet on its outstretched muzzle. Obviously, stronger measures were called for. That's when I arrived on the scene.

Jonesboro is not quite like anyplace else on earth. It's a beautiful little town nestled in the wooded valleys of East Tennessee. It was once the capital of the lost state of Franklin, was home to a scrappy young lawyer by the name of Andy Jackson and now, after 200 years, is one of the best preserved towns of its kind anywhere. No power or telephone lines ensnare its streets, no parking meters clutter its curbs and old-fashioned street lamps cast a warm glow on brick-paved sidewalks.

On the town square is the county courthouse, where dwell Jonesboro's pigeons. Though completed in 1912 it is still called the "new" courthouse by most of Jonesboro's citizens who well remember the "old" courthouse, and probably the one before that.

Stray dogs, camels and pack mules eventually find their way home, and it is no different with wandering Jonesboro-ites. After several years of living in the West and exploring lands far beyond, I returned to Jonesboro to spend my declining years near the poor dirt farm where I grew up.

Citizens of Jonesboro seldom leave town except in a state of acute disgrace, so it was naturally assumed when I left that there must have been substantial reason. This meant I was eyed with some suspicion when I reappeared on the village green. But I opened up a downtown office just as bold as brass, looked up old girlfriends and settled back in place as easily as a pup taking a nap. Whatever crimes or indiscretions that vivid imaginations may have conjured to account for my departure were apparently forgotten.

It was a comfortable reunion but alas, too good to last. When I moved into my second-story office directly across from the courthouse and laid eyes on all those grinning pigeons lined up on the balcony I knew fate had caught up with me.

No one could dispute that the courthouse needed to be rid of the pigeons, and it was equally clear that the only way to do it was to shoot them. Their clock-tower fortress was apparently impregnable to all other forms of attack. But until my arrival no one had possessed both the will and the means of dealing with them. My office window provided the perfect sniper's roost. Destiny surely planned the whole thing.

As discreetly as enthusiasm permitted, I passed the word that I wouldn't mind taking a few potshots at the pests "just to keep my eye in practice." And just as discreetly the word came back that it was my "bound civic duty to rid the town of the damnable beasts." Even the sheriff, H. H. Hackmore, who is in charge of courthouse maintenance, stopped by to bestow his blessing.

Second only to the speed of light is the blazing speed of Jonesboro gossip. In no time at all everyone knew that a big-game hunter had come to do in the courthouse pigeons.

The distance to the peak of the clock tower was 41 yards, and the choice of weapons was my old pump-up pellet rifle. I figured this was the only safe equipment for the job even though it might handicap me a bit. I didn't know just how much of a handicap this rifle would be until I tried adjusting the aperature sight for a 41-yard dead-on point of impact. The pellets hit everywhere except dead-on, with the group sizes ranging upwards of 12 inches.

I'd made the mistake of announcing that I would begin knocking off the pigeons on the following Monday morning. I say mistake because when I arrived at my office opposite the courthouse, pellet rifle in hand, a crowd of onlookers had already gathered in the street. It was going to be a memorable day in Jonesboro, they reckoned, and they wanted to see it happen. There was a smattering of applause as I entered the ancient building, and I heard Harry Weems, who runs Harry's Men's Shop downstairs, offering to cover all bets. I wish I could forget the whole thing.

Filling the rifle's air reservoir with 10 full strokes of the pump handle, I fed a pellet into the chamber, and taking a rest on the window sill, leveled the sights on a particularly plump pigeon. The crowd below held its breath. *Plufft* went the air rifle, *splat* went the wayward pellet on an ornate piece of concrete scroll work, *coo* went the pigeon. I'd missed clean. A chuckle ripped through the throng.

Feverishly I pumped the rifle and fed another pellet. *Plufft, splat, coo.* The chuckle became a collective guffaw. *Plufft, splat, coo*; again and again I tried. No results. "Hey Carmichel," someone shouted from below, "if them was lions they'd be pickin' their teeth about now." *Plufft, splat, coo.* Even the pigeons joined in the fun, waddling over to the roof's edge for a better view of the whole sorry spectacle.

By then my audience was drifting off by twos and threes, telling each other it was the biggest disappointment since Jack Hicks' hanging was called off in the spring of 1904. Harry Weems paid off his losses and my disgrace was thus complete.

That day I called Robert Beeman, the country's leading dealer and importer of quality air rifles and accessories, and ordered a German-made Feinwerkbau Model 124 air rifle and a supply of special pointed pellets. The FWB-124 is the hottest thing going in hunting-type air rifles. It gives a muzzle velocity of better than 800 feet per second (close on to a .22 Rimfire Short) and is accurate enough to hit a dime--or a pigeon's head--at 41 yards. "Send it airmail," I told him. "I've got to salvage my reputation."

Revenge would be mine, I told everyone, describing the fancy new air rifle I'd ordered. But sometimes the airmails fly slowly, and it was weeks before the FWB-124 arrived. By then the whole town was laughing about the "wonderful pigeon gun" that existed only in my imagination.

But it did arrive, and my first few test shots showed it was more accurate than I had dared hope. Topped off with a 10X scope and zeroed dead on at 41 yards, it cut a neat little group about the size of a shirt button.

The next morning a small crowd of onlookers gathered to watch the next chapter in Carmichel's disgrace. Even the pigeons seemed interested, and about 20 lined up on the balcony railing to see what was happening. I started on the right end of the row and worked my way to the left.

The first bird toppled off with scarcely a flutter. Its neighbor noted its demise with idle curiosity but no particular concern. When the next two or three went over the edge the others began to get somewhat curious about what was happening and cooed at the stricken forms with some amazement. In fact, as more pigeons fell, the remainder reacted with increasing amazement, those on the left end having to lean far out from their perches, wings aflutter, in order to watch the peculiar behavior of the brethren.

The first run was 14 straight kills with Harry collecting bets like mad. The pigeons still hadn't figured out what was going on, but apparently they thought it best to go somewhere else and give it some thought. That day's tally was 27 pigeons and a few stray starlings. Next day would be even better.

But next day disaster arrived in a totally unexpected form. I was brewing a pot of tea and had just killed the first pigeon when "Shorty" Howze, Jonesboro's seven-foot policeman, charged into my office and presented me with an official complaint lodged by one of the townspeople. According to the unnamed plaintiff, I was "molesting Jonesboro's beloved pigeons."

"C'mon, Shorty," I protested, "you've got to be kidding. Everybody wants rid of those pigeons. You told me so yourself. And besides, I have the sheriff's O.K."

"I know," Shorty replied. "The courthouse is county property and you can shoot over there all you want to. But the chief says when you shoot across the street you're violating Jonesboro air space. So the complaint stands."

"Who complained?" I asked.

"I'm not allowed to say."

"I know, but tell me anyway."

"That crazy-acting woman that just moved into the old Crookshanks place."

"The one that has all the cats and makes her husband walk the dog at two in the morning?"

"That's the one."

"Thanks for telling me."

"By the way," he said, stopping at the door and glancing at the air rifle by the window, "that's one hell of a pigeon gun."

Except for an occasional guarded shot, the rifle stood unused. The pigeons flourished and grew fatter, and life in Jonesboro trudged through an uneventful winter. By spring I'd all but forgotten the ill-fated affair when a really splashing event brought the pigeon problem back into brilliant focus. The leading character was none other than one Judge Hiram Walpole Justice. It seemed that Judge Justice, all decked out in his new tailor-made blue suit, had just handed down an important decision and was on the courthouse lawn discussing it with some reporters when a pigeon swooped down and scored a bull's-eye on his jacket. Thousands saw it live on TV.

The judge turned on his heel and stalked back into the courthouse, muttering something about the futility of "holding court in a chicken house." That afternoon Judge Justice was in my office learning the finer points of shooting courthouse pigeons with a FWB-124.

Every morning thereafter, the judge would declare a recess at about 10 o'clock and rush over to my office to blast a few pigeons, giggling fiendishly every time one plopped on the pavement. Hizzoner became a *very* fine marksman.

This had been going on for about two weeks when one morning Shorty, backed up by the mayor and two constables, crashed into my office and waved a warrant at the backside of the judge. "Aha," yelled the mayor. "We know what you've been up to, Carmichel. This time we've got you dead to rights."

With his judicially-robed backside to the door, the judge was kneeling on the floor and taking a careful aim with the rifle resting on the windowsill. So intent was he that he didn't even look up.

"That ain't me," I said, stepping out of the washroom. "That's Judge Justice. And if I was you I wouldn't bother him right now."

All worthy projects must end, and by late summer the judge and I had pretty well wiped out the pigeon population, firing something near 1,500 pellets in the process. In all probability the whole thing would have reached a happy conclusion had it not been for one of those freak, clod-dissolving August cloudbursts. The creek overflowed its banks, poured into the streets of Jonesboro, and for the first time in history, flooded the courthouse basement where two hundred years of moldy Jonesboro records are kept. The devastation to the voting records in particular was total. Wiped out.

An official inquiry was launched in order to discover the cause of the unprecedented flooding, and the final ruling was:

"One Jim Carmichel, a citizen of Jonesboro, is known to have shot pigeons on the courthouse roof and thereby stopped up the gutters and drainpipes, thus contributing to the flooding."

There's a new crop of pigeons living in the clock tower now. I can see them looking this way. ...

(All statements of fact in the story you have just read have been checked and found accurate. Certain names and dates have, however, been altered to protect wrongdoers.--Ed.)

15

THE WARWICK WOODLANDS

By Frank Forester

It's hard to say who started writing outdoor literature, but one would be hard put to claim that Frank Forester didn't have something to do with it in a big way. His real name was Henry William Herbert, but millions of readers only knew him as Frank Forester. Most of his work appeared in the mid-1850s. I can't think of too many outdoor writers who can claim that sort of longevity. Read this and you'll know why.

Much as I had heard of Tom Draw, I was, I must confess, taken altogether aback when I, for the first time, set eyes upon him. I had heard Harry Archer talk of him fifty times as a crack shot; as a top sawyer at a long day's fag; as the man of all others he would choose as his mate, if he were to shoot a match, two against two-- what then was my astonishment at beholding this worthy, as he reared himself slowly from his recumbent position? It is true, I had heard his sobriquet, "Fat Tom," but, Heaven and Earth! Such a mass of beef and brandy as stood before me, I had never even dreamt of. About five feet six inches at the very utmost in the perpendicular, by six or--"by'r lady"--nearer seven in circumference, weighing, at the least computation, two hundred and fifty pounds, with a broad jolly face, its every feature--well formed and handsome, rather than otherwise--mantling with an expression of the most perfect excellence of heart and temper, and over-shadowed by a

129

vast mass of brown hair, sprinkled pretty well with gray! Down he plumped from the counter with a thud that made the whole floor shake, and with a hand outstretched, that might have done for a Goliath, out he strode to meet us.

"Why, hulloa! hulloa! Mr. Archer," shaking his hand till I thought he would have dragged the arm clean out of the socket-- "How be you, boy? How be you?"

"Right well, Tom, can't you see? Why confound you, you've grown twenty pounds heavier since July!--but here, I'm losing all my manners!--this is Frank Forester, whom you have heard me talk about so often! He dropped down here out of the moon, Tom, I believe! at least I thought about as much of seeing the man in the moon, as of meeting *him* in this wooden country--but here he is, as you see, come all the way to take a look at the natives. And so, you see, as you're about the greatest curiosity I know of in these parts, I brought him straight up here to take a peek! Look at him, Frank-- look at him well! Now, did you ever see, in all your life, so extraordinary an old devil?--and yet, Frank, which no man could possibly believe, the old fat animal had some good points about him--he can walk *some* shoot, as he says, *first best*! and drink--good Lord, how he can drink!"

"And that reminds me" exclaimed Tom, who with a ludicrous mixture of pleasure, bashfulness, and mock anger, had been listening to what he evidently deemed a high encomium; "that *we* haven't drinked yet; have you quit drink, Archer, since I was to York? What'll you take, Mr. Forester? Gin? yes, I have got some prime gin! You never sent me up them groceries though, Archer; well, then, here's luck! What, Yorkshire, is that you? I should ha' thought now, Archer, you'd have cleared that lazy Injun out afore this time!"

"Whoy, measter Draa--what 'na loike's that kind o'talk?-- coom coom now, where'll Ay tak t'things tull?"

"Put Mr. Forester's box in the bedroom of the parlor--mine upstairs, as usual," cried Archer. Look sharp and get the traps out. Now, Tom, I suppose you have got no supper for us?"

"Cooper, Cooper! you snooping little devil," yelled Tom, addressing his second hope, a fine dark-eyed, bright-looking lad of ten or twelve years; Don't you see Mr. Archer's come?--away with you and light the parlor fire, look smart now, or I'll cure you!

Supper--you're always eat! eat! eat! or, drink! Drink!--*drunk!* Yes!
supper; we've got pork! and chickens--"

"Oh! damn your pork," said I, "salt as the ocean I suppose!"
"And double damn your chickens," chimed in Harry, "old
superannuated cocks which must be caught *now,* and then beheaded,
and then soused into hot water to fetch off the feathers; and save
you lazy devils the trouble of picking them. No, now, Tom! get us
some fresh meat for tomorrow; and for tonight let us have some hot
potatoes, and some bread and butter, and we'll find beef; eh,
Frank? and now look sharp, for we must be up in good time
tomorrow, and, to be so, we must to bed betimes. And now, Tom,
are there any cock?"

"Cock! yes, I guess there be, and quail, too, pretty plenty! quite
a smart chance of them, and not a shot fired among them this fall,
anyhow!"

"Well, which way must we beat tomorrow? I calculate to shoot
three days with you here; and, on Wednesday night, when we get in,
to hitch up and drive into Sullivan, and see if we can't get a deer or
two! You'll go, Tom?"

"Well, well, we'll see anyhow; but for tomorrow, why, I guess
we must beat the 'Squire's swamp hole first; there's ten or twelve
cock there, I know; I see them there myself last Sunday; and then
acrost them buckwheat stubbles, and the big bog meadow, there's
a *drove* of quail there; two or three bevys got in one, I reckon;
leastwise I counted thirty-three last Friday was a week; and through
Seer's big swamp, over to the great spring!"

"How *is* Seer's swamp? too wet, I fancy," Archer interposed,
"at least I noticed, from the mountain, that all the leaves were
changed in it, and that the maples were quite bare."

"Pretty fair, pretty fair, I guess," replied stout Tom, "I harnt
been there myself though, but Jem was down with the hounds arter
an old fox t'other day, and sure enough *he said* the cock kept
flopping up quite thick afore him; but then the critter *will* lie,
Harry; he *will* lie like thunder, you know; but somehow I concaits
there be cock there too; and then, as I was saying, we'll stop at the
great spring and get a bit of summat, and then beat Hell Hole;
you'll have sport there for sartin! What dogs have you got with you,
Harry?"

"Your old friends, *Shot* and *Chase,* and a couple of spaniels for thick covert!"

"Now, gentlemen, your suppers are all ready."

"Come, Tom," cried Archer; "you must take a bite with us-- Tim, bring us in three bottles of champagne, and lots of ice, do you hear?"

And the next moment we found ourselves installed in a snug parlor, decorated with a dozen sporting prints, a blazing hickory fire snapping and sputtering and roaring in a huge Franklin stove; our luggage safely stowed in various corners, and Archer's double gun case propped on two chairs below the window.

An old-fashioned round table, covered with clean white linen of domestic manufacture, displayed the noble round of beef which we had brought up with us, flanked by a platter of magnificent potatoes, pouring forth volumes of dense steam through the cracker in their dusky skins; a lordly dish of butter, than might have pleased the appetite of *Sisera*; while eggs and ham, and pies of apple, mincemeat, cranberry, and custard, occupied every vacant space, save where two ponderous pitchers, mantling with ale and cider, and two respectable square bottles, labelled "Old Rum" and "Brandy--1817," relieved the prospect. Before we had sat down, Timothy entered, bearing a horse bucket filled to the brim with ice, from whence protruded the long necks and split corks of three champagne bottles.

"Now, Tim," said Archer, "get your own supper, when you've finished with the cattle; feed the dogs well tonight; and then to bed. And hark you, call me at five in the morning; we shall want you to carry the game bag and the drinkables; take care of yourself, Tim, and good night!"

"No need to tell him that," cried Tom, "he's something like yourself; I *tell* you, Archer, if Tim ever dies of thirst, it must be where there is nothing wet but water!"

"Now hark to the old scoundrel, Frank," said Archer, "hark to him pray, and if he doesn't out eat both of us, and outdrink anything you ever saw, may I miss my first bird tomorrow--that's all! Give me a slice of beef, Frank; that old Goth would cut it in an inch thick, if I let him touch it; out with a cork, Tom! Here's to our sport tomorrow!"

"Uh; that goes good!" replied Tom, with an oath, which, by the apparent gusto of the speaker, seemed to betoken that the wine had tickled his palate--"that goes good! that's different from the darned red trash you left up here last time"

"And of which you have *left* none, I'll be bound," answered Archer, laughing; my best Latour, Frank, which the old infidel calls trash."

"It's all below, every bottle of it," answered Tom: "I wouldn't use such rotgut stuff, no, not for vinegar. 'Taint half so good as that red sherry you had up here oncet; that was poor weak stuff, too, but it did well to make milk punch of; it did well instead of milk."

"Now, Frank," said Archer, "you won't believe me, *that I know*; but it's true, all the same. A year ago, this autumn, I brought up five gallons of exceedingly stout, rather fiery, young, grown sherry--draught wine, you know!--and what did Tom do here, but mix it, half and half, with brandy, nutmeg, and sugar, and drink it for milk punch!"

"I did *so,* by the eternal," replied Tom, bolting a huge lump of beef, in order to enable himself to answer--"I did *so,* and good milk punch it made, too, but it was too weak! Come, Mr. Forester, we harn't drinked yet, and I'm kind o' gittin dry!"

And now the mirth waxed fast and furious--the champagne speedily was finished, the supper things cleared off, hot water and Starke's Ferintosh succeeded, cheroots were lighted, we drew closer in about the fire, and, during the circulation of two tumblers--for to this did Harry limit us, having the prospect of unsteady hands and aching head before him for the morrow--never did I hear more genuine and real humor, than went round our merry trio.

Tom Draw, especially, though all his jokes were not such altogether as I can venture to insert in my chaste paragraphs, and though at times his oaths were too extravagantly rich to brook repetition, shone forth resplendent. No longer did I wonder at what I had before deemed Harry Archer's strange hallucination; Tom Draw *is* a decided genius--rough as a pine knot in his native woods--but full of mirth, of shrewdness, of keen mother wit, of hard horse sense, and last, not least, of the most genuine milk of human kindness. He is a rough block; but as Harry says, there is solid timber under the uncouth bark enough to make five hundred men, as men go now-a-days *in cities!*

At ten o'clock, thanks to the excellent precautions of my friend Harry, we were all snugly berthed before the whiskey, which had well justified the high praise I had heard lavished on it, had made any serious inroads on our understanding, but not before we had laid in a *quantum* to ensure a good night's rest.

Bright and early was I on foot the next day, but before I had half dressed myself I was assured, by the clatter of the breakfast things, that Archer had again stolen a march upon me; and the next moment my bedroom door, driven open by the thick boot of that worthy, gave me a full view of his person--arrayed in a stout fustian jacket--with half a dozen pockets in full view, and Heaven only knows how many more lying *perdu* in the broad skirts. Kneebreeches of the same material, with laced half boots and leather leggins, set off his stout calf and well-turned ankles.

"Up! up! Frank," he exclaimed, "it is a morning of ten thousand; there has been quite a heavy dew, and by the time we are afoot it will be well evaporated; and then the scent will lie, I promise you! make haste, I tell you, breakfast is ready!"

Stimulated by his hurrying voice, I soon completed my toilet, and entering the parlor found Harry busily employed in stirring to and fro a pound of powder on one heated dinner plate, while a second was undergoing the process of preparation on the hearthstone under a glowing pile of hickory ashes.

At the side table, covered with guns, dog whips, nipple wrenches, and the like, Tim, rigged like his master, in half boots and leggins, but with a short roundabout of velveteen, in place of the full-skirted jacket, was filling our shot pouches by aid of a capacious funnel, more used, as its odor betokened, to facilitate the passage of gin or Jamaica spirits than of so sober a material as cold lead.

At the same moment entered mine host, togged for the field in a huge pair of cowhide boots, reaching almost to the knee, into the tops of which were tucked the lower ends of a pair of trousers, containing yards enough of buffalo cloth to have eked out the mainsail of a North River sloop; a waistcoat and single-breasted jacket of the same material, with a fur cap, completed his attire; but in his hand he bore a large decanter filled with a pale yellowish liquor, embalming a dense mass of fine and wormlike threads, not very different in appearance from the best vermicelli.

"Come, boys, come--here's your bitters," he exclaimed; and, as if to set the example, filled a big tumbler to the brim, gulped it down as if it had been water, smacked his lips, and incontinently tendered it to Archer, who, to my great amazement, filled himself likewise a more moderate draught, and quaffed it without hesitation.

"That's good, Tom," he said, pausing after the first sip; "that's the best I ever tasted here; how old's that?"

"Five years!" Tom replied: "five years last fall! Daddy Tom made it out of my own best apples--take a horn, Mr. Forester," he added, turning to me-- "It's *first best* cider sperits--better a darned sight than that Scotch stuff you make such an etarnal fuss about, toting it up here every time, as if we'd nothing fit to drink in the country!"

And to my sorrow I did taste--old apple whiskey, with Lord knows how much snakeroot soaked in it for five years! They may talk about gall being bitter; but, by all that's wonderful, there was enough of the *amari aliquid* in this *fonte,* to me by no means of *leporum,* to have given an extra touch of bitterness to all the gall beneath the canopy; and with my mouth puckered up, till it was like anything on earth but a mouth, I set the glass down on the table; and for the next five minutes could do nothing but shake my head to and fro like a Chinese mandarin, amidst the loud and prolonged roars of laughter that burst like thunderclaps from the huge jaws of Thomas Draw, and the subdued and half-respectful cachinnations of Tim Matlock.

By the time I had got a little better, the black tea was ready, and with thick cream, hot buckwheat cakes, beautiful honey, and--as a stand by--the still venerable round, we made out a very tolerable meal.

This done, with due deliberation Archer supplied his several pockets with their accustomed load--the clean-punched wads in this--in that the Westley Richards' caps--here a pound horn of powder--there a shot-pouch on Skye's lever principle, with double mouthpiece--in another, screwdriver, nipple wrench, and the spare cones; and, to make up the tale, dog whip, dram bottle, and silk handkerchief in the sixth and last.

"Nothing like this method in the world," said Harry, clapping his low-crowned broad-brimmed mohair cap upon his head; "take my word for it. Now, Tim, what have you got in the bag!"

"A bottle of champagne, sur," answered Tim, who was now employed slinging a huge fustian game bag, with a net-work front, over his right shoulder, to counterbalance two full shot belts which were already thrown across the other--"a bottle of champagne, sur--a cold roast chicken--t' Cheshire cheese--and t' pilot biscuits. Is your dram bottle filled wi' t' whiskey, please sur?"

"Aye, aye, Tim. Now let loose the dogs--carry a pair of couples and a leash along with you; and mind you, gentlemen, Tim carries shot for all hands; and luncheon--but each one finds his own powder, caps, etc.; and any one who wants a dram, carries his own--the devil a-one of you gets a sup out of my bottle, or a charge out of my flask! That's right, old Trojan, isn't it? with a good slap on Tom's broad shoulder.

"Shot! Shot--why Shot! don't you know me old dog? cried Tom, as the two setters bounded into the room, joyful at their release--"good dog! good Chase!" feeding them with great lumps of beef.

"Avast! there Tom--have done with that," cried Harry; "you'll have the dogs so full that they can't run."

"Why, how'd you like to hunt all day without your breakfast--hey?"

"Here, lads! here, lads! wh-e-ew!" and followed by his setters, with his gun under his arm, away went Harry; and catching up our pieces likewise, we followed, nothing loth, Tim bringing up the rear with the two spaniels fretting in their couples, and a huge black thorn cudgel, which he had brought, as he informed me, "all t' way from bonny Cawoods."

It was as beautiful a morning as ever lighted sportsmen to their labors. The dew, exhaled already from the long grass, still glittered here and there upon the shrubs and trees, though a soft fresh southwestern breeze was shaking it thence momently in bright and rustling showers; the sun, but newly risen, and as yet partially enveloped in the thin gauzelike mists so frequent at that season, was casting shadows, seemingly endless, from every object that intercepted his low rays, and checkering the whole landscape with that play of light and shade, which is the loveliest accessory to a lovely scene; and lovely was the scene, indeed, as e'er was looked upon by painter's or by poet's eye--how then should humble prose do justice to it?

Seated upon the first slope of a gentle hill, midway of the great valley heretofore described, the village looked due south, toward the chains of mountains which we had crossed on the preceding evening, and which in that direction bounded the landscape. These ridges, cultivated halfway up their swelling sides, which lay mapped out before our eyes in all the various beauty of orchards, yellow stubbles, and rich pastures dotted with sleek and comely cattle, were rendered yet more lovely and romantic by here and there a woody gorge, or rocky chasm, channeling their smooth flanks and carrying down their tributary rills to swell the main stream at their base. Toward these we took our way by the same road which we had followed in an opposite direction on the previous night--but for a short space only--for having crossed the stream by the same bridge which we had passed on entering the village, Tom Draw pulled down a set of bars to the left, and strode out manfully into the stubble.

"Hold up, good lads!--whe-ew--whewt!" and away went the setters through the moist stubble, heads up and sterns down, like foxhounds on a breast-high scent, yet under the most perfect discipline; for at the very first note of Harry's whistle, even when racing at the top of their pace, they would turn simultaneously, alter their course, cross each other at right angles, and quarter the whole field, leaving no foot of ground unbeaten.

No game, however, in this instance, rewarded their exertions; and on we went across a meadow, and two other stubbles, with the like result. But now we crossed a gentle hill, and at its base came on a level tract, containing at the most 10 acres of marsh land, overgrown with high coarse grass and flags. Beyond this, on the right, was a steep rocky hillock, covered with tall and thrifty timber of some 30 years' growth, but wholly free from underwood, sumach and birch, with a few young oak trees interspersed; but in the middle of the swampy level, covering at most some five or six acres, was a dense circular thicket composed of every sort of thorny bush and shrub, matted with catbriers and wild vines, and overshadowed by a clump of tall and leafy ashes, which had not as yet lost one atom of their foliage, although the underwood beneath them was quite sere and leafless.

"Now then," cried Harry, "this is the `Squire's swamp hole!" Now for a dozen cock! hey, Tom! Here, couple up the setters, Tim; and let the spaniels loose. Now Flash! now Dan! down, charge, you little villains!" and the well-broke brutes dropped on the instant. "How must we beat this cursed hole!"

"You must go through the very thick of it, concarn you!" exclaimed Tom; "at your old work already, hey? trying to shirk at first!"

"Don't swear so! you old reprobate! I know my place, depend on it," cried Archer; "but what to do with the rest of you!--there's the rub!"

"Not a bit of it, " cried Tom--"here, Yorkshire--Ducklegs--here, what's your name--get away you with those big dogs--atwixt the swamp hole, and the brush there by the fence, and look out that you mark every bird to an inch! You, Mr. Forester, go in there, under that butternut' you'll find a blind track there, right through the brush--keep that `twixt Tim and Mr. Archer; and keep your eyes skinned, do! there'll be a cock up before you're ten yards in. Archer, you'll go right through, and I'll--"

"You'll keep well forward on the right--and mind that no bird crosses to the hill; we never get them, if they once get over. All right! In with you now! Steady, Flash! steady! hie up, Dan!" and in a moment Harry was out of sight among the brushwood, though his progress might be traced by the continual crackling of the thick underwood.

Scarce had I passed the butternut, when, even as Tom had said, up flapped a woodcock scarcely ten yards before me, in the open path, and rising heavily to clear the branches of a tall thornbush, showed me his full black eye, and tawny breast, as fair a shot as could be fancied.

"Mark!" halloaed Harry to my right, his quick ear having caught the flap of the bird's wing, as he rose. "Mark cock--Frank!"

Well--steadily enough, as I thought, I pitched my gun up! covered my bird fairly! pulled!--the trigger gave not to my finger. I tried the other. Devil's in it, I had forgot to cock my gun! and ere I could retrieve my error, the bird had topped the bush, and dodged out of sight, and off--Mark! Mark!--Tim! I shouted.

"Ey! ey! sur--Ay see's um!"

"Why, how's that, Frank?" cried Harry. "Couldn't you get a shot?"

"Forgot to cock my gun!" I cried; but at the selfsame moment the quick sharp yelping of the spaniels came on my ear. "Steady, Flash! Steady, sir! Mark!" But close upon the word came the full round report of Harry's gun. "Mark! again!" shouted Harry, and again his own piece sent its loud ringing voice abroad. "Mark! now a third! Mark, Frank!"

And as he spoke I caught the quick rush of his wing, and saw him dart across a space, a few yards to my right. I felt my hand shake; I had not pulled a trigger in ten months, but in a second's space I rallied. There was an opening just before me between a stumpy thick thornbush which had saved the last bird and a dwarf cedar; it was not two yards over; he glanced across it; he was gone, just as my barrel sent its charge into the splintered branches.

"Beautiful!" shouted Harry, who, looking through a cross glade, saw the bird fall, which I could not. "Beautiful shot, Frank! Do all your work like that, and we'll get twenty couple before night!"

Have I killed him!" answered I, half doubting if he were not quizzing me.

"Killed him? of course you have; doubled him up completely! But look sharp! there are more birds before me! I can hardly keep the dogs down, now! There! there goes one--clean out of shot of me, though! Mark! mark, Tom! Gad, how the fat dog's running!" he continued. "He sees him! Ten to one he gets him! There he goes--bang! A long shot, and killed clean!"

"Ready!" cried I. "I'm ready, Archer!"

"Bag your bird, then. He lies under that dock leaf, at the foot of yon red maple! That's it; you've got him. Steady now, till Tom gets loaded!"

"What did you do?" asked I. "You fired twice, I think!"

"Killed two!" he answered. "Ready, now!" and on he went, smashing away the boughs before him, while ever and anon I heard his cheery voice, calling or whistling to his dogs, or rousing up the tenants of some thickets into which even he could not force his way; and I, creeping, as best I might among the tangled brush, now plunging half thigh deep in holes full of tenacious mire, now blundering over the moss-covered stubs, pressed forward, fancying every instant that the rustling of the briers against my jacket was the flip-flap of a rising woodcock. Suddenly, after bursting through a mass of thorns and wild vine, which was in truth almost impassable, I came upon a little grassy spot quite clear of trees, and covered with the tenderest verdure, through which a narrow rill stole silently; and as I set my first foot on it, up jumped, with his beautiful variegated back all reddened by the sunbeams, a fine and full-fed woodcock, with the peculiar twitter which he utters when surprised. He had not gone ten yards, however, before my gun was at my shoulder and the trigger drawn; before I heard the crack I saw him cringe; and, as the white smoke drifted off to leeward, he fell heavily, completely riddled by the shot, into the brake before me; while at the same moment, whir-r-r! up sprung a bevy of twenty quail, at least, startling me for the moment by the thick whirring of their wings, and skirring over the underwood right toward Archer. "Mark, quail!" I shouted, and, recovering instantly my nerves, fired my one remaining barrel after the last bird! It was a long shot, yet I struck him fairly, and he rose instantly right upward, towering high! high! into the clear blue sky, and soaring still, till his life left him in the air, and he fell like a stone, plump downward!

"Mark him! Tim!"

"Ey, ey! sur. He's a dead-un, that's a sure thing!"

At my shot all the bevy rose a little, yet altered not their course the least, wheeling across the thicket directly round the front of Archer, whose whereabouts I knew, though I could neither see nor hear him. So high did they fly that I could observe them clearly, every bird well defined against the sunny heavens. I watched them eagerly. Suddenly one turned over; a cloud of feathers streamed off down the wind; and then, before the sound of the first shot had reached my ears, a second pitched a few yards upward, and after a heavy flutter, followed its hapless comrade.

Turned by the fall of the two leading birds, the bevy again wheeled, still rising higher, and now flying very fast; so that, as I saw by the direction which they took, they would probably give Draw a chance of getting in both barrels. And so indeed it was; for, as before, long ere I caught the booming echoes of his heavy gun, I saw two birds keeled over, and almost at the same instant, the cheery shout of Tim announced to me that he had bagged my towered bird! After a little pause, again we started, and hailing one another now and then, gradually forced our way through brake and brier toward the outward verge of the dense covert. Before we met again, however, I had the luck to pick up a third woodcock, and as I heard another double shot from Archer, and two single bangs from Draw, I judged that my companions had not been less successful than myself. At last, emerging from the thicket, we all converged, as to a common point, toward Tim; who, with his game bag on the ground, with its capacious mouth wide open to receive our game, sat on a stump with the two setters at a charge beside him.

"What do we score?" cried I, as we drew near. "What do we score?"

"I have four woodcocks, and a brace of quail," said Harry.

"And I, two cock and a brace," cried Tom, "and missed another cock; but he's down in the meadow here, behind that 'ere stump alder!"

"And I, three woodcock and one quail!" I chimed in, naught abashed.

"And Ay'se marked doon three woodcock--two more beside yon big un, that measter Draa made siccan a bungle of--and all t' quail--every feather on um--doon i' t' bog meadow yonner--ooh! but we'se make grand sport o't!" interposed Tim, now busily employed stringing bird after bird up by the head, with loops and buttons in the game bag!"

"Well done then, all!" said Harry. "Nine timberdoodles and five quail, and only one-shot missed! That's not bad shooting, considering what a hole it is to shoot in. Gentlemen, here's your health," and filling himself out a fair-sized wine-glass-full of Ferintosh, into the silver cup of his dram bottle, he tossed it off; and then poured out a similar libation for Tim Matlock. Tom and myself, nothing loth, obeyed the hint, and sipped our modicums of distilled waters out of our private flasks.

"Now, then," cried Archer, "let us pick up these scattering birds. Tom Draw, you can get yours without a dog! And now, Tim, where are yours?"

"T' first lies oop yonner in yon boonch of brachens, ahint t' big scarlet maple; and t' other--"

"Well! I'll go to the first. You take Mr. Forester to the other, and when we have bagged all three, we'll meet at the bog meadow fence, and then hie at the bevy!"

This job was soon done, for Draw and Harry bagged their birds cleverly at the first rise; and although mine got off at first without a shot, by dodging round a birch tree straight in Tim's face, and flew back slap toward the thicket, yet he pitched in its outer skirt, and as he jumped up wild I cut him down with a broken pinion and a shot through his bill at fifty yards, and Chase retrieved him well.

"Cleverly stopped, indeed!" Frank halloaed; "and by no means an easy shot! and so our work's clean done for this place, at the least!"

"The boy *can* shoot *some*," observed Tom Draw, who loved to bother Timothy; "the boy *can* shoot *some,* though he *does* come from Yorkshire!"

"Gad! and Ay wush Ay'd no but gotten thee i' Yorkshire, measter Draa!" responded Tim.

"Why! what if you had got me there?"

"What? Whoy, Ay'd clap thee iv a cage, and hug thee round t' feast and fairs loike; and shew thee to folks at so mooch a head. Ay'se sure Ay'd mak a fortune o' t!"

"He has you there, Tom! Ha! ha! ha!" laughed Archer. "Tim's down upon you there, by George! Now, Frank, do fancy Tom Draw in a cage at Boroughbridge or Catterick fair! Lord! how the folks would pay to look at him! Fancy the sign board too! The Great American Man-Mammoth! Ha! ha! ha! But come, we must not stay here talking nonsense, or we shall do no good. Show me, Tim, where are the quail!"

"Doon i' t' bog meadow yonner! joost i' t' slack, see thee, there!" pointing with the stout black-thorn; "amang yon bits o' bushes!"

"Very well--that's it; now let go the setters; take Flash and Dan along with you, and cut across the country as straight as you can go the the spring head, where we lunched last year; that day, you know, Tom, when McTavish frightened the bull out of the meadow, under the pin oak tree. Well! put the champagne into the spring to cool, and rest yourself there till we come; we shan't be long behind you."

Away went Tim, stopping from time to time to mark our progress, and over the fence into the bog meadow we proceeded; a rascally piece of broken tussocky ground, with black mud knee-deep between the hags, all covered with long grass. The third step I took, over I went upon my nose, but luckily avoided shoving my gun barrels into the filthy mire.

"Steady, Frank, steady! I'm ashamed of you!" said Harry; so hot and so impetuous; and your gun too at the full cock; that's the reason, man, why you missed firing at your first bird, this morning. I never cock either barrel till I see my bird; and, if a bevy rises, only one at a time. The birds will lie like stones here; and we cannot walk too slow. Steady, Shot, have a care sir!"

Never, in all my life, did I see anything more perfect than the style in which the setters drew those bogs. There was no more of racing, no more of impetuous dash; it seemed as if they knew the birds were close before them. At a slow trot, their sterns whipping their flanks at every step, they threaded the high tussocks. See! the red dog straightens his neck, and snuffs the air.

"Look to! look to, Frank! they are close before old Chase!"

Now he draws on again, crouching close to the earth. "Toho! Shot!"

Now he stands! no! no! not yet--at least he is not certain! He turns his head to catch his master's eye! Now his stern moves a little; he draws on again.

There! he is sure now! what a picture--his black full eye intently glaring, though he cannot see anything in that thick mass of herbage; his nostril wide expanded, his lips slavering from intense excitement; his whole form motionless, and sharply drawn, and rigid, even to the straight stern and lifted foot, as a block wrought to mimic life by some skillful sculptor's chisel; and, scarce ten yards behind, his liver-colored comrade backs him--as firm, as stationary, as immovable, but in his attitude, how different! Chase feels the hot scent steaming up under his very nostril; feels it in every nerve, and quivers with anxiety to dash on his prey, even while perfectly restrained and steady. Shot, on the contrary, though a few minutes since he too was drawing, knows nothing of himself, perceives no indication of the game's near presence, although improved by discipline, his instinct tells him that his mate has found them. Hence the same rigid form, still tail, and constrained attitude, but in his face--for dogs *have* faces--there is none of that tense energy, that evident anxiety; there is not frown upon his brow, no glare in his mild open eye, no slaver on his lip!

"Come up, Tom; come up, Frank, they are all here; we must get in six barrels; they will not move; come up, I say!"

And on we came, deliberately prompt, and ready. Now we were all in line: Harry the center man, I on the right, and Tom on the left hand. The attitude of Archer was superb; his legs set a little way apart, as firm as if they had been rooted in the soil; his form drawn back a little, and his head erect, with his eye fixed upon the dogs; his gun held in both hands, across his person, the muzzle slightly elevated, his left grasping the trigger guard; the thumb of the right resting upon the hammer, and the forefinger on the trigger of the left-hand barrel; but, as he had said, neither cocked. "Fall back, Tom, if you please, five yards or so," he said, as coolly as if he were unconcerned, "and you come forward, Frank, as many; I want to drive them to the left, into those low red bushes; that will do: now then, I'll flush them; never mind me, boys, I'll reserve my fire."

And, as he spoke, he moved a yard or two in front of us, and under his very feet, positively startling me by their noisy flutter, up sprang the gallant bevy: fifteen or sixteen well-grown birds, crowding and jostling one against the other. Tom Draw's gun, as I well believe, was at his shoulder when they rose; at least his first shot was discharged before they had flown half a rood, and of course harmlessly: the charge must have been driven through them like a single ball; his second barrel instantly succeeded, and down came two birds, caught in the act of crossing. I am myself a quick shot, *too* quick if anything, yet my first barrel was exploded a moment after Tom Draw's second; the other followed, and I had the satisfaction of bringing both my birds down handsomely; then up went Harry's piece--the bevy being now twenty or twenty-five yards distant--cocking it as it rose, he pulled the trigger almost before it touched his shoulder, so rapid was the movement; and, though he lowered the stock a little to cock the second barrel, a moment scarcely passed between the two reports, and almost on the instant two quail were fluttering out their lives among the bog grass.

Dropping his butt, without a word, or even a glance to the dogs, he quietly went on to load; nor indeed was it needed: at the first shot they dropped into the grass, and there they lay as motionless as if they had been dead, with their heads crouched between their paws; nor did they stir thence till the tick of the gunlocks announced that we again were ready. Then lifting up their heads, and rising on their forefeet, they sat half-erect, eagerly waiting for the signal:

"Hold up, good lads!" and on they drew, and in an instant pointed on two several birds. "Fetch!" and each brought his burthen to our feet; six birds were bagged at that rise, and thus before eleven o'clock we had picked up a dozen cock, and within one of the same number of fine quail, with only two shots missed. The poor remainder of the bevy had dropped, singly, and scattered, in the red bushes, whither we instantly pursued them, and where we got six more, making a total of seventeen birds bagged out of a bevy twenty strong at first.

One towered bird of Harry's certainly killed dead, we could not with all our efforts bring to bag; one bird Tom Draw missed clean, and the remaining one we could not find again; another dram of whiskey, and into Seer's great swamp we started: a large piece of woodland, with every kind of lying. At one end it was open, with soft black loamy soil, covered with docks and coltsfoot leaves under the shade of large but leafless willows, and here we picked up a good many scattered woodcock; afterward we got into the heavy thicket with much tangled grass, wherein we flushed a bevy, but they all took to tree, and we made very little of them; and here Tom Draw began to slow and and labor; the covert was too thick, the bottom too deep and unsteady for him.

Archer perceiving this, sent him at once to the outside; and three times, as we went along, ourselves moving nothing, we heard the round reports of his large caliber. "A bird at every shot, I'd stake my life," said Harry, "he never misses cross shots in the open;" at the same instant a tremendous rush of wings burst from the heaviest thicket: "Mark! partridge! partridge!" and as I caught a glimpse of a dozen large birds fluttering up, one close upon the other, and darting away as straight and nearly as fast as bullets, through the dense branches of a cedar brake, I saw the flashes of both Harry's barrels, almost simultaneously discharged, and at the same time over went the objects of his aim; but ere I could get up my gun the rest were out of sight. "You must shoot, Frank, like lightning, to kill these beggars; they are the ruffed grouse, though they call them partridge here; see! are they not fine fellows?"

Another hour's beating, in which we still kept picking up, from time to time, some scattering birds, brought us to the spring head, where we found Tim with luncheon ready, and our fat friend reposing at his side, with two more grouse, and a rabbit which he had bagged along the covert's edge. Cool was the Star champagne; and capital was the cold fowl and Cheshire cheese; and most delicious was the repose that followed, enlivened with gay wit and free good humor, soothed by the fragrance of the exquisite cheroots, moistened by the last drops of the Ferintosh qualified by the crystal waters of the spring. After an hour's rest, we counted up our spoil; four ruffed grouse, nineteen woodcocks, with ten brace and a half of quail beside the bunny, made up our score--done comfortably in four hours.

"Now we have finished for today with quail," said Archer, "but we'll get full ten couple more of woodcock; come, let us be stirring; hang up your game bag in the tree, and tie the setters to the fence; I want you in with me to beat, Tim; you two chaps must both keep the outside--you all the time, Tom; you, Frank, till you get to that tall thunder-shivered ash tree; turn in there, and follow up the margin of a wide slank you will see; but be careful, the mud is very deep, and dangerous in places; now then, here goes!"

And in he went, jumping a narrow streamlet into a point of thicket, through which he drove by main force. Scarce had he got six yards into the brake, before both spaniels quested; and, to my no small wonder, the jungle seemed to come alive with woodcock; eight or nine, at the least, flapped up at once, and skimmed along the tongue of the coppice toward the high wood, which ran along the valley, as I learned afterward, for full three miles in length-- while four or five more wheeled off to the sides, giving myself and Draw fair shots, by which we did not fail to profit; but I confess it was with absolute astonishment that I saw two of those turned over, which flew inward, killed by the marvelously quick and unerring aim of Archer, where a less thorough sportsman would have been quite unable to discharge a gun at all, so dense was the tangled jungle. Throughout the whole length of the skirt of coppice, a hundred and fifty yards, I should suppose at the utmost, the birds kept rising as it were incessantly--thirty-five, or, I think, nearly forty, being flushed in less than twenty minutes, although comparatively few were killed, partly from the difficulty of the ground, and partly from their getting up by fours and fives at once. Into the high wood, however, at the last we drove them; and there, till daylight failed us, we did our work like men. By the cold light of the full moon we wended homeward, rejoicing in the possession of twenty-six couple and a half of cock, twelve brace of quail--we found another bevy on our way home and bagged three birds almost by moonlight--five ruffed grouse, and a rabbit. Before our wet clothes were well changed, supper was ready, and a good blowout was followed by sound slumbers and sweet dreams, fairly earned by nine hours of incessant walking.

BASS SERIES LIBRARY
by Larry Larsen

(BSL1) FOLLOW THE FORAGE VOL. 1 - BASS/PREY RELATIONSHIP - Learn how to determine dominant forage in a body of water and you will consistently catch more and larger bass.

(BSL2) VOL. 2 BETTER BASS ANGLING TECHNIQUES - Learn why one lure or bait is more successful than others and how to use each lure under varying conditions.

(BSL3) BASS PRO STRATEGIES - Professional fishermen know how changes in pH, water level, temperature and color affect bass fishing, and they know how to adapt to weather and topographical variations. Learn from their experience. Your productivity will improve after spending a few hours with this compilation of techniques!

(BSL4) BASS LURES - TRICKS & TECHNIQUES - When bass become accustomed to the same artificials and presentations seen over and over again, they become harder to catch. You will learn how to modify your lures and rigs and how to develop new presentation and retrieve methods to spark the interest of largemouth!

(BSL5) SHALLOW WATER BASS - Bass spend 90% of their time in the shallows, and you spend the majority of the time fishing for them in waters less than 15 feet deep. Learn productive new tactics that you can apply in marshes, estuaries, reservoirs, lakes, creeks and small ponds, and you'll likely triple your results!

(BSL6) BASS FISHING FACTS - Learn why and how bass behave during pre- and post-spawn, how they utilize their senses when active and how they respond to their environment, and you'll increase your bass angling success! By applying this knowledge, your productivity will increase for largemouth as well as redeye, Suwannee, spotted and other bass species!

(BSL7) TROPHY BASS - If you're more interested in wrestling with one or two monster largemouth than with a "panful" of yearlings, then learn what techniques and locations will improve your chances. This book takes a look at geographical areas and waters that offer better opportunities to catch giant bass. You'll also learn proven lunker-bass-catching techniques for both man-made and natural bodies of water!

(BSL8) ANGLER'S GUIDE TO BASS PATTERNS - Catch bass every time out by learning how to develop a productive pattern quickly and effectively. "Bass Patterns" is a reference source for all anglers, regardless of where they live or their skill level. Learn how to choose the right lure, presentation and habitat under various weather and environmental conditions!

(BSL9) BASS GUIDE TIPS - Learn secret techniques known only in a certain region or state that often work in waters all around the country. It's this new approach that usually results in excellent bass angling success. Learn how to apply what the country's top guides know!

Nine Great Volumes To Help You Catch More and Larger Bass!

LARSEN ON BASS SERIES

(LB1) LARRY LARSEN ON BASS TACTICS is the ultimate "how-to" book that focuses on proven productive methods. It is dedicated to serious bass anglers - those who are truly interested in learning more about the sport and in catching more and larger bass each trip. Hundreds of highlighted tips and drawings explain how you can catch more and larger bass in waters all around the country. This reference source by America's best known bass fishing writer will be invaluable to both the avid novice and expert angler!

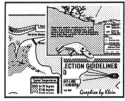

BASS WATERS SERIES
by Larry Larsen

Take the guessing game out of your next bass fishing trip. The most productive bass waters in each Florida region are described in this multi-volume series, including boat ramps, seasonal tactics, water characteristics and much more. Both popular and overlooked locations are detailed with numerous maps and photos. The author has lived and fished extensively in each region of the state over the past 25 years.

(BW1) GUIDE TO NORTH FLORIDA BASS WATERS - Covers from Orange Lake north and west. Includes Lakes Orange, Lochloosa, Talquin and Seminole, the St. Johns, Nassau, Suwannee and Apalachicola Rivers and many more of the region's best! You'll learn where bass bite in Keystone Lakes, Newnans Lake, St. Mary's River, Doctors Lake, Black Creek, Juniper Lake, Ortega River, Lake Jackson, Lake Miccosukee, Chipola River, Deer Point Lake, Blackwater River, Panhandle Mill Ponds and many more!

(BW2) GUIDE TO CENTRAL FLORIDA BASS WATERS - Covers from Tampa/Orlando to Palatka. Includes Lakes George, Rodman, Monroe, Tarpon and the Harris Chain, the St. Johns, Oklawaha and Withlacoochee Rivers and many others! You'll find the best spots to fish in the Ocala Forest, Crystal River, Hillsborough River, Conway Chain, Homosassa River, Lake Minneola, Lake Weir, Lake Hart, Spring Runs and many more!

(BW3) GUIDE TO SOUTH FLORIDA BASS WATERS - Covers from I-4 to the Everglades. Includes Lakes Tohopekaliga, Kissimmee, Okeechobee, Poinsett, Tenoroc and Blue Cypress, the Winter Haven Chain and many more! You'll learn where bass can be caught in Fellsmere Farm 13. Caloosahatchee River, Lake June-in-Winter, Lake Hatchineha, the Everglades, Lake Istokpoga, Peace River, Crooked Lake, Lake Osborne, St. Lucie Canal, lake Trafford, Shell Creek, Lake Marian, Myakka River, Lake Pierce, Webb Lake and many more!

> For more than 20 years, award-winning author Larry Larsen has studied and written about bass fishing. His angling adventures are extensive, from Canada to Honduras and from Cuba to Hawaii. He is Florida Editor for *Outdoor Life* and contributor to all major outdoor magazines.

OUTDOOR TRAVEL SERIES
by Larry Larsen and M. Timothy O'Keefe

Candid guides with inside information on the best charters, time of the year, and other important recommendations that can make your next fishing and/or diving trip much more enjoyable.

(OT1) FISH & DIVE THE CARIBBEAN - Vol. 1 Northern Caribbean, including Cozumel, Cayman Islands, The Bahamas, Jamaica, Virgin Islands and other popular destinations. Required reading for fishing and diving enthusiasts who want to know the most cost-effective means to enjoy these Caribbean islands. You'll learn how to select the best destination and plan appropriately for your specific interests.

(OT3) FISH & DIVE FLORIDA & The Keys - Includes in-depth information on where and how to plan a vacation to America's most popular fishing and diving destination. Special features include artificial reef loran numbers; freshwater springs/caves; coral reefs/barrier islands; gulf stream/passes; inshore flats/channels; and back country estuaries.

(OT2) FISH & DIVE THE CARIBBEAN - Vol. 2 - *COMING SOON!* Southern Caribbean, including Guadeloupe, Costa Rica, Venezuela, other destinations.

"Fish & Dive the Caribbean, Vol. 1" was one of four finalists in the Best Book Content Category of the National Association of Independent Publishers 1991 competition. Over 500 books were submitted by various U.S. publishers, including Simon & Schuster and Turner Publishing, Inc. Said the NAIP judges "An excellent source book with invaluable instructions for fishing or diving. Written by two nationally-known experts who, indeed, know what vacationing can be!"

DIVING SERIES
by M. Timothy O'Keefe

(DL1) DIVING TO ADVENTURE will inform and entertain novice and experienced divers alike with its in-depth discussion of how to get the most enjoyment from diving and snorkeling. Aimed at divers around the country, the book shows how to get started in underwater photography, how to use current to your advantage, how to avoid seasickness, how to dive safely after dark, and more. Special sections detail how to plan a dive vacation, including live-aboard diving.

M. Timothy O'Keefe was editor of the first major dive travel guidebook published in the U.S. The award-winning author writes for numerous diving, travel and sportfishing publications.

COASTAL FISHING GUIDES

(FG1) FRANK SARGEANT'S SECRET SPOTS - Tampa Bay to Cedar Key - A unique "where-to" book of detailed secret spots for Florida's finest saltwater fishing. This guide book describes little-known honeyholes and tells exactly how to fish them. Prime seasons, baits and lures, marinas and dozens of detailed maps of the prime spots are included. A comprehensive index helps the reader to further pinpoint productive areas and tactics.

(FG2) FRANK SARGEANT'S SECRET SPOTS -Southwest Florida
COMING SOON!!

INSHORE SERIES

by Frank Sargeant

(IL1) THE SNOOK BOOK-"Must" reading for anyone who loves the pursuit of this unique sub-tropic species. Every aspect of how you can find and catch big snook is covered, in all seasons and all waters where snook are found.

(IL2) THE REDFISH BOOK-Packed with expertise from the nation's leading redfish anglers and guides, this book covers every aspect of finding and fooling giant reds. You'll learn secret techniques revealed for the first time. After reading this informative book, you'll catch more redfish on your next trip!

(IL3) THE TARPON BOOK-Find and catch the wily "silver king" along the Gulf Coast, north through the mid-Atlantic, and south along Central and South American coastlines. Numerous experts share their most productive techniques.

(IL4) THE TROUT BOOK-Jammed with tips from the nation's leading trout guides and light tackle anglers. For both the old salt and the rank amateur who pursue the spotted weakfish, or seatrout, throughout the coastal waters of the Gulf and Atlantic.

Frank Sargeant is a renown outdoor writer and expert on saltwater angler. He has traveled throughout the state and Central America in pursuit of all major inshore species. Sargeant is Outdoor Editor of the Tampa Tribune and a Senior Writer for *Southern Saltwater* and *Southern Outdoors* magazines.

HUNTING LIBRARY

by John E. Phillips

(DH1) MASTERS' SECRETS OF DEER HUNTING - Increase your deer hunting success significantly by learning from the masters of the sport. New information on tactics and strategies for bagging deer is included in this book, the most comprehensive of its kind.

(DH2) THE SCIENCE OF DEER HUNTING - Covers why, where and when a deer moves and deer behavior. Find the answers to many of the toughest deer hunting problems a sportsman ever encounters!

(TH1) MASTERS' SECRETS OF TURKEY HUNTING - Masters of the sport have solved some of the most difficult problems you will encounter while hunting wily longbeards with bows, blackpowder guns and shotguns. Learn the 10 deadly sins of turkey hunting and what to do if you commit them.

FISHING LIBRARY

(CF1) MASTERS' SECRETS OF CRAPPIE FISHING by John E. Phillips - Learn how to make crappie start biting again once they have stopped, how to select the color of jig to catch the most and biggest crappie, how to find crappie when a cold front hits and how to catch them in 100-degree heat as well as through the ice. Unusual but productive crappie fishing techniques are included. Whether you are a beginner or a seasoned crappie fisherman, this book will improve your catch!

OUTDOOR ADVENTURE LIBRARY

by Vin T. Sparano, Editor-in-Chief, Outdoor Life

(OA1) HUNTING DANGEROUS GAME -It's a special challenge to hunt dangerous game - those dangerous animals that hunt back! Live the adventure of tracking a rogue elephant, surviving a grizzly attack, facing a charging Cape buffalo and driving an arrow into a giant brown bear at 20 feet. These classic tales will make you very nervous next time you're in the woods!

(OA2) GAME BIRDS & GUN DOGS - A unique collection of stories about hunters, their dogs and the upland game and waterfowl they hunt. These tales are about those remarkable shots and unexplainable misses. You will read about good gun dogs and heart-breaking dogs, but never about bad dogs, because there's no such animal.

LARSEN'S OUTDOOR PUBLISHING

CONVENIENT ORDER FORM

BASS SERIES LIBRARY ($11.95 ea.
or $79.95 for autographed set)
___ 1. Better Bass Angling Vol 1
___ 2. Better Bass Angling Vol 2
___ 3. Bass Pro Strategies
___ 4. Bass Lures Tricks/Techniques
___ 5. Shallow Water Bass
___ 6. Bass Fishing Facts
___ 7. Trophy Bass
___ 8. Bass Patterns
___ 9. Bass Guide Tips

INSHORE LIBRARY ($11.95 ea.
or $35.95 for autographed set)
___ IL1. The Snook Book
___ IL2. The Redfish Book
___ IL3. The Tarpon Book
___ IL4. The Trout Book

COASTAL FISHING GUIDES
($14.95)
___ FG1.Sargeant's Secret Spots -
Tampa Bay/Cedar Key

BASS WATERS SERIES ($14.95 ea.
or $37.95 autographed set)
___ BW1. Guide/North Fl. Bass Waters
___ BW2. Guide/Cntrl Fl. Bass Waters
___ BW3. Guide/South Fl. Bass Waters

LARSEN ON BASS SERIES ($14.95)
___ LB1. Larry Larsen on Bass Tactics

OUTDOOR TRAVEL SERIES
($13.95 ea.)
___ OT1. Fish & Dive The Caribbean
___ OT3. Fish & Dive Florida/ Keys

DIVING SERIES ($11.95)
___ DL1. Diving to Adventure

**HUNTING LIBRARIES/FISHING
LIBRARIES** ($11.95 ea.)
___ DH1. Mstrs' Secrets/ Deer Hunting
___ DH2. Science of Deer Hunting
___ TH1. Mstrs' Secrets/ Turkey Hunting
___ OA1.Hunting Dangerous Game!
___ OA2.Game Birds & Gun Dogs
___ CF1. Mstrs' Secrets /Crappie Fishing

> **BIG SAVINGS!**
> 2-3 books, discount 10%
> 4 or more books, discount 20%

> **FOREIGN ORDERS**
> Please send check in U.S. funds
> drawn on a U.S. bank and add $2
> per book for airmail rate

ALL PRICES INCLUDE POSTAGE/HANDLING

No. of books _____ *x $*_____ *each = $*_____
No. of books _____ *x $*_____ *each = $*_____
No. of books _____ *x $*_____ *each = $*_____
 Multi-book Discount **(%)**   *$*_____

TOTAL ENCLOSED (check or money order)   *$*_____

*NAME*_____ *ADDRESS*_____

*CITY*_____ *STATE*_____ *ZIP*_____

Send check or Money Order to: *Larsen's Outdoor Publishing, Dept. RD93*
2640 Elizabeth Place, Lakeland, FL 33813

We'll send this brochure free to a friend:
*Friend's name*_____ *Address*_____
*City*_____ *State*_____ *Zip*_____

WRITE US!

If our books have helped you be more productive in your outdoor endeavors, we'd like to hear from you! Let us know which book or series has strongly benefited you and how it has aided your success or enjoyment. We'll listen.

We also might be able to use the information in a future book. Such information is also valuable to our planning future titles and expanding on those already available.

Simply write to Larry Larsen, Publisher, Larsen's Outdoor Publishing, 2640 Elizabeth Place, Lakeland, FL 33813.

We appreciate your comments!

Larry Larsen

OUTDOOR SPORTS SHOWS, CLUB SEMINARS and IN-STORE PROMOTIONS

Over the course of a year, most of our authors give talks, seminars and workshops at trade and consumer shows, expos, book stores, fishing clubs, department stores and other places. Please try to stop by and say hi to them. Bring your book by for an autograph and some information on secret new hot spots and methods to try. At these events, we always have our newest books, so come and check out the latest information. If you know of an organization that needs a speaker, contact us for information about fees. We can be reached at 813-644-3381. At our autograph parties, we talk "outdoors" and how to enjoy it to the fullest!

Save Money On Your Next Outdoor Book!

Because you've purchased a Larsen's Outdoor Publishing Book, you can be placed on our growing list of **preferred customers.**

You can receive special discounts on our wide selection of Outdoor Libraries and Series, written by our expert authors.

PLUS...

Receive Substantial Discounts for Multiple Book Purchases

AND...

Advance notices on upcoming books!

Yes, put my name on your mailing list to receive

1. Advance notice on upcoming outdoor books
2. Special discount offers

Name_____

Address_____

City, State, Zip_____

VIN T. SPARANO BOOKS
SPECIALIZING IN CLASSIC OUTDOOR LITERATURE
ORDER FORM

_____ Hunting Dangerous Game, by Vin T. Sparano $9.95
_____ Game Birds And Gun Dogs, by Vin T. Sparano $9.95
_____ Tears & Laughter, by Gene Hill $14.95
_____ Hell, I Was There, by Elmer Keith............. .... $24.95
_____ Sheep and Sheep Hunting, by Jack O'Connor...... .... $35.00
_____ Horn Of the Hunter, by Robert Ruark............ .... $35.00
_____ The Old Man And The Boy & The Old
      Man's Boy Grows Older, by Robert Ruark........ .... $17.95
_____ Use Enough Gun, by Robert Ruark............. .... $32.50
_____ Ruark's Africa, by Robert Ruark............. .... $30.00
_____ Karamojo Safari, by W.D.M. Bell............. .... $24.95
_____ Bell of Africa, by W.D.M. Bell............. .... $24.95
_____ Classic Hunting Tales, by Vin T. Sparano............ .... $19.95
_____ Complete Outdoors Encyclopedia, by Vin T. Sparano..... .... $39.95
_____ Tales of Woods and Waters, by Vin T. Sparano.......... .... $37.00
_____ Pastimes of an American Hunter, by Theodore Roosevelt............ $16.95
_____ African Game Trails, by Theodore Roosevelt............ .... $19.95
_____ River Gods and Spotted Devils, by Sporting Classics.... .... $14.95
_____ Danger, by Ben East.................. .... $15.95
_____ Narrow Escapes, by Ben East.................. .... $15.95
_____ The Outdoor Life Bear Book, by Chet Fish.............. .... $26.95
_____ Best of Zane Grey, Hunting and Fishing Tales.......... .... $16.95
_____ The Wild Bears, by George Laycock................ .... $19.95
_____ Pondoro, The Last of the Ivory Hunters,
      by John (Pondoro) Taylor.................. .... $30.00
_____ Death in the Long Grass, by Peter Capstick.......... .... $17.95
_____ Death in the Dark Continent, by Peter Capstick....... .... $14.95
_____ Death in the Silent Places, by Peter Capstick........ .... $15.95
_____ The Man-Eaters of Tsavo, by Lt. Col. J.H. Patterson... .... $14.95
_____ African Hunter, by Baron Bror Von Blixen-Finecke..... .... $14.95

         Postage and Handling: $2.50 per book........... .... _____
                         TOTAL............ .... _____

Name_____
Address_____
City_____State_____Zip_____

Copy this page and mail to:
Vin T. Sparano Books, Dept. LL
17 Henning Drive, Fairfield, NJ 07004

COVER PAINTING

Courtesy Of Robert K. Abbett and Wild Wings, Inc., Lake City, MN 55041; 612/345-5355.

Robert Abbett is one of America's contemporary art masters in the genre of outdoor art and he is most at home painting the scenes of sporting dogs, flyfishing, western life and portraits for which he is so well known. His works appear in museum exhibits country wide. As the country's foremost sporting dog artist, Bob is widely appreciated for his ability to paint each dog as an individual, placing it naturally into an authentic background.